Everything 101

Everything 101

A COMPLETE EDUCATION IN A SNAP

Lisa Sonne

FALL RIVER PRESS

Fall River Press
122 Fifth Avenue
New York, NY 10011

ISBN: 978-1-4351-2059-4

Printed and bound in China

1 3 5 7 9 10 8 6 4 2

The information in this book has been drawn from many sources
and is assumed to be accurate. Although every effort has been made to verify
the information, the publishers cannot guarantee its perfect accuracy.

Photo Credits: © Didier Descouens: 93; © David Gaya: 79 (3); © André Gunthert: 26; © Bobak Ha'Eri: 18;
Zachary Harden: 83 (bottom icon); © Hans Hillewaert: 11; iStockphoto.com: All design elements, unless
otherwise noted; 135; © Devorah Klein: 16; John F. Kennedy Presidential Library and Museum, Boston:
30 bottom, Ernest Hemingway Photograph Collection; Library of Congress: 12, 25, 28, 29, 30 top, 104; 67,
Carol Highsmith; Maria Mann: Illustrations on 39, 44, 46, 48 (middle), 109, 114, 119, 120, 121 (bottom), 122;
NASA: 99, 111; Marie-Lan Nguyen: 14, 79 (7), 129; © Andreas Praefcke: 74, 79 (2); Private Collection:
34 (middle and right); © Bill Rankin: 21, 88; © Andrea Selby: Illustrations on 71, 101; © Bjørn Christian
Tørrissen: 17; © François Trazzi: 79 (6); U.S. Army: 113; United States Central Intelligence Agency: 117;
© William Warby: 79 (5); © Philipp Weissenbacher: 79 (1); Wikimedia Commons: 34 left, 45, 47, 57 (both),
60, 63, 64, 65, 70, 71, 79 (4), 95, 97, 106, 110, 123

DEDICATION

To Ann Miriam Vierhus Sonne and Roscoe Newbold Sonne, Jr.
Dedicated with love, gratitude, and admiration to my remarkable
parents who raised four kids to value creativity, curiosity, and
questions, and to love words, work, and wonder.

Each managed to have successful careers, while still making
family dinner together with real conversation a priority. They
showed us that both books and the real world are playgrounds
and schools for all of us. They continue to make laughter
and love a part of any "curriculum" and gathering.

And to Victor Dorff, my dear husband
who makes everything better!

ACKNOWLEDGMENTS

For this little book of eclectic and eccentric knowledge, big thanks go to
the wonderful people at Fall River Press: Andrea Rotondo opened the door,
Heather Rodino helped launch and develop the project, Devorah Klein carried
the editing, fact checking, and production baton to the end, Lindsay Herman
copyedited, and the design team of Kevin Ullrich, Jo Obarowski,
Maria Mann, and Wendy Fields made it look this good!

Big thanks also to the teachers, librarians, webmasters, writers, and resource
makers who provide huge wells of information and insights for dipping.
My cups are running over, and all the gratitude doesn't fit here.

CONTENTS

Arts 101 62

Social Studies 101 80

Science 101 96

Philosophy & Religion 101

Bonus Chapter:
Psychology 101

Appendix:
Answers

Introduction 101

THIS IS A LITTLE BOOK WITH A BIG AIM: TO ENLARGE YOUR KNOWLEDGE and tickle your imagination. Whether you want a sneak start on a fuller education, plan to win *Jeopardy!* someday, or are a baby boomer exercising your brain, here are eight different subject areas primed for treasure hunting.

Like the 101 introductory survey classes at universities and colleges, *Everything 101* offers some helpful general knowledge. Also, like the best moments of late-night dorm conversations, you may glean some totally useless but incredible facts—and laugh at truths odder than fiction.

Did you know that Benjamin Franklin sometimes wrote while naked? What would you say are some of the most "sacred" places on the planet? Is a shooting star a meteor or a meteorite? And what is "opportunity cost," anyway?

This little volume isn't comprehensive or encyclopedic. It's, after all, a welcoming, 100-level book, meant to whet your appetite. Consider this a pupu platter of knowledge nuggets, little tapas of trivia, savvy sips to slake a thirst. Well, you get the idea.

Think of the table of contents as your course catalog. Choose which "classes" you want to take and when. It's *your* curriculum. Read the chapters in order, or skip around. Ditch one section, and highlight another. Each section has some basics, some **fyi** notecards, and good reference material, balanced with goofy trivia, cool visuals, and extra credit challenges. (No worries: answers are in the back.)

More good news: no finals, no tuition, no homework, and you grade yourself!

Whether you want to feel smart ("I knew that!") or be smarter ("Good to know!"), dig in for some fun.

History 101

HIS-STORY OR HER-STORY, THE "NONFICTION" ACCOUNTS OF HUMANITY, are our universal legacy, the road map in the rearview mirror of our social and political travels, the narrative of the evolution of human constructs, the . . . Well, you get the idea, right?

Studying history is more than memorizing dates and slogging through battles and proper names. History provides the human "before" for the "after" we are in, whether you are looking back as a military strategist, a psychoanalyst, a drama fiend, a scholar, or a weekend wonderer.

The lessons to cull from the mistakes and marvels of mankind exceed any one book's chapter or person's lifetime, but that doesn't mean you can't learn a little now.

What did the indigenous Americans contribute that probably affects you every day? What's cool about the Khmer civilization and hot about the Hammurabi Code? Which president added the most states to the United States? And what does the color purple have to do with history? The answers to these questions and many more are recorded somewhere in the annals of history, as well as in this chapter.

Weighty Words in History

Some aspects of human existence haven't changed all that much in the last four or five thousand years. People were rich and poor, leaders and followers, the rulers and the ruled. Whether on stone, animal skins, or paper, some of the recorded words that have survived the ages give us insights into our past and present.

The Code of Hammurabi

The code of laws of the Babylonian King Hammurabi dates back to 1790 BCE. The inscribed stone, or stele, discovered in 1901 is more than seven feet long, with over 280 laws in the vernacular language of Akkadian. Originally, the stone tablet was on display in a public place in ancient Babylon. Now, it's on exhibit at the Louvre Museum in Paris. A frieze on the U.S. Supreme Court Building includes an image of Hammurabi, honoring his place among the lawmakers of old.

{ **fyi** }

Two systems for chronicling the major eras of human history are BC/AD and BCE/CE. CE stands for "Common Era" and is equivalent in historic dates to AD (Anno Domini, or "the year of our Lord"). BCE is the equivalent of BC ("Before Christ") and stands for "Before Common Era," "Before Christian Era," or "Before Current Era" (take your pick).

   Both systems—BC/AD and BCE/CE—are based on a sixth-century calculation of the year Jesus was born, which has since been determined to be incorrect by several years. The starting year for AD and CE were kept the same to prevent us all from going AWOL.

The Rosetta Stone

The stone did not become famous for the text on its surface. Sure, it's nice to read about all the good things Ptolemy did for the temples, but what really makes the Rosetta Stone important is its value as a translation tool. Dated to around 196 BCE, the Rosetta Stone contains multilingual inscriptions of the same text—in ancient Greek, in Demotic, and in Egyptian hieroglyphs. Those hieroglyphs had fallen into such disuse by the eighteenth century that scholars hadn't been able to translate the tales and warnings on many Egyptian archeological finds. When a soldier in Napoleon's army discovered the Rosetta Stone in 1799, some smart guys got to work

The Rosetta Stone: Promoting foreign languages since before the Common Era.

comparing the languages, and finally, voilà, hieroglyphs became readable again, opening up the world to more ancient Egyptian history.

The Dead Sea Scrolls

These scrolls include about nine hundred documents and fragments on parchment and papyrus written in Hebrew, Greek, and Aramaic. Some scrolls were texts of the Hebrew Bible; others were historic records. They date back to about one hundred years before and after the start of the Common Era, but the invaluable documents weren't found until the mid-twentieth century (between 1947 and 1956) in eleven caves near the northwest shore of the Dead Sea. The historical scrolls mostly contain information about community rules and war conduct.

The Dead Sea Scrolls were written in Hebrew, Greek, and Aramaic.

How Old is Ancient?

What does "ancient" mean anyway? You may have aunts, childhood books, and family stories that seem "ancient." In historical terms, though, "ancient" refers to much older times—roughly from the beginning of recorded human history to an end-time that is a little more vague. For Western history, the fall of the Western Roman Empire in 476 CE is often used as the endpoint, but some scholars refer to the rise of Islam as a terminating point for "ancient history" (about 700 CE), and still others use the year 1000 CE and the middle of the Middle Ages. Chinese history usually cuts off "ancient history" at the Imperial Age, which began around 200 BCE.

The Magna Carta

An important step toward a constitutional monarchy in England and an early milestone toward the Constitution of the United States, the Magna Carta was signed reluctantly in 1215 by the English King John, then modified several times during the next decade. The document lessened the power of the monarchy, granting greater rights and freedoms to a larger number of people. The Magna Carta was written in Latin, and the title translates to "Great Charter."

Martin Luther's Ninety-Five Theses

These were essentially a list of grievances, written in 1517, that criticized the practices of the Catholic Church, including the act of selling "indulgences" (which waived or reduced punishments for some sins). In fact, the full name of Luther's document was *The Ninety-Five Theses on the Power and Efficacy of Indulgences*. The printing press allowed copies to be distributed quickly, first throughout Germany, and eventually throughout the rest of Europe. Luther's "protest" is credited with sparking the "Protest"-ant Reformation, a movement that altered the course of history in Europe and triggered the migrations of people to the Americas.

Five of the Great Civilizations

You've heard of the ancient Greek and Roman civilizations in Europe, and of the Incan, Aztec, and Mayan empires in South America. Here are five other important cultures that left their marks and monuments on human history and deserve to be in your memory bank.

Sixty Seconds for the Summation of Sumerian Civilization

You could say time, transportation, and even history all began with the Sumerians.

Six thousand years ago, the Sumerians emerged in the Euphrates and Tigris River plain, developing from a priesthood-led temple culture to become military rulers, until they were conquered in 2000 BCE. They were "ancient" even to the Babylonians. Stone tablets with the first

Sumerian stone tablet.

written language (cuneiform) are credited to the Sumerians, as well as record keeping. If *pre-history* is defined as "before written records," then it can be said that "history" began with the Sumerians.

The concepts of sixty minutes in an hour and sixty seconds in a minute also came from the Sumerians, as well as twenty-four hours in a day.

Say thanks to Sumerians, also, for the wheel (first used as pottery kick-wheels, then developed for transportation), as well as for the use of the plow and large-scale agriculture, and for key advances in mathematics. City-state government seems to be another Sumerian invention.

{ fyi }

The Sumerian language is an orphan—unique, with no other relatives in its family tree. It is agglutinating, meaning the language is designed around suffixes and prefixes added to core words. The Hungarian and Finnish languages are also agglutinating.

Hooked on Phoenicians

The Phoenicians are credited with being the first sailors, explorers, pirates, and navigators of the world. Motivated by curiosity and commerce, they developed trading networks between the years 1550 and 300 BCE. They established ports all around the Mediterranean, from Cypress to Sicily to the Iberian Peninsula and northern Africa, and even ventured into the raucous Atlantic Ocean. The Phoenicians are also said to have had the first written alphabet, which they spread to other regions. The Greeks absorbed the alphabet, which they, in turn, spread to the Romans and Etruscans.

Scholars, from archaeologists to geneticists, debate the origin of the Phoenicians. Were they descendents of the Canaanites? The invading "Sea Peoples?" Their name is believed to be derived from the ancient Greek word for "purple." The Phoenicians manufactured and traded a Tyrian purple powder—a unique source of the color—something the upper levels of Greek society greatly desired for their clothes, since purple was a symbol of luxury and power. The dye was made from the mucus of murex seashells, once abundant in the Mediterranean.

The Byzantine Byzantine Empire

For most people, the term *byzantine* means complicated, intricate, and maybe even devious—whether it's describing your tax form or a piece of legislation. For more than one thousand years, the Byzantine (with a capital "B") Empire was one of the dominant forces in Europe. It wasn't called Byzantine at the time, though. It was variously known as the Eastern Roman Empire or the Greek Empire. The people called themselves Romans, but spoke Greek. How byzantine is that?

At one time, the Empire included parts of the Middle East, northern Africa, and southern and eastern Europe. For this civilization, the *alpha* was about 330 CE, when the Roman emperor Constantine the Great overtook the city of Byzantium on the Bosphorus and renamed it Constantinople. The *omega* was 1453, when the Ottoman Turks commandeered Constantinople and declared it to be Istanbul.

Religious art, literature, and architecture attest to the Christian influence and great talents in the Byzantine Empire, which was an economic and

The Hagia Sophia in Istanbul, Turkey.

political powerhouse for a millennium. The Hagia Sophia in Istanbul, once the largest cathedral in the world, remains as an architectural marvel and a marker of history in this now predominantly Islamic part of the world.

Caring About the Khmer

The world's largest religious building (Angkor Wat) and other architectural gems are the surviving mementos of an artistic Asian civilization that thrived from the ninth to fourteenth century using clever irrigation, reservoirs, and moats to increase crop productivity. With enhanced nutrition and prosperity, the Khmer, or Angkor, civilization flourished in the region north of the great Tonle Sap Lake—in what is now Cambodia and part of Thailand, Vietnam, and Laos.

Rather than focus on conquering the world (like many other civilizations did), the Khmer's religious ruling class of "God Kings" supported the arts and often employed thousands of dancers, musicians, and artisans. Different theories explain the decline of the empire, including drought, changing religions, and the ironic fact that the roads they built for successful trade expansion provided a way for invaders and conquerors to enter their jungled realm.

The Khmer civilization was not well known globally until the vine-covered ruins were visited in 1860 by a French botanist, whose accounts excited European imaginations and prompted restoration work. The contents of the

Khmer libraries had decomposed by then; most of their literature was written on leaves and animal skins, but the magnificent stone carvings on the buildings speak of a sophisticated culture with strong influences from both Hinduism and Buddhism.

Angkor Wat in Cambodia was rediscovered in 1860.

Modern Khmer

The Khmer language endures as the official language spoken in Cambodia today. Glimpses of the Khmer civilization can also be seen in the faces of contemporary Cambodians and in the revival of the arts in areas like Siem Reap. The brutality of the communist Khmer Rouge (Red Khmer) led by Pol Pot in the 1970s gave "Khmer" a bad name, left deep scars, and kept the area closed from the world until 1990.

Now visitors to the region are welcome to see the giant stone heads at the Banyon Temple of Angkor Thom, the long tableaus of more than two thousand apsaras (female dancers and angels) in Angkor Wat, and the Sanskrit inscriptions on the rose-colored Banteay Srei, a tenth century temple. Continual restoration is underway on dozens of sites.

Monte Albán in Oaxaca, Mexico, is one of the earliest cities of Mesoamerica.

The Zip of Zapotec

Not unlike the Khmer, the Zapotec civilization of the Americas is also memorialized by its intriguing stone edifices, surviving language, and the faces of local people today. Their terraced pyramids, ball courts, tombs, and temples near Oaxaca, Mexico, are still dramatic reminders of a culture that flourished alongside the Mayans.

The Zapotecs had developed advanced agricultural techniques, great jewelry craftsmanship (especially with gold), and a written language based on a glyph for each syllable.

These Meso-American people thrived from about 500 BCE to 1000 CE and were still strong when Europeans arrived in the middle of the sixteenth century, despite battles with the Aztecs in the late fifteenth and early sixteenth centuries. The Spaniards conquered the Zapotecs and converted many to Catholicism, away from their polytheist beliefs in deities, including the Rain God and the God of Light.

The architectural and cultural Zapotec achievements of Monte Albán (the capital city) and Mitla are compelling tourist draws even today, 1,500 years later. The descendents of the indigenous Zapotec still live in Mexico, as well as in areas like Los Angeles and California's Central Valley, keeping the Zapotec language alive.

Foods for Historic Thought

Where would Irish history be without the potato? Who would Italians be without tomatoes? And what would *any* of us do without chocolate?

None of those foods—or tobacco, chewing gum, chili peppers, or corn— were part of European, Asian, or African diets until the "discovery" of the new world. After 1492, as a result of the introduction of foods from North and South America, nutrition in Europe improved and changed population growth rates, economies, and history.

Foods and tasty treats of the Americas include:

- avocado
- baked clams
- beans (more than a dozen varieties)
- chewing gum
- chocolate
- corn
- cranberries
- maple sugar and syrup
- melons (including watermelon)
- nuts (including walnuts and peanuts)

- peppers
- popcorn
- potatoes (white and sweet)
- pumpkins
- squash
- sunflower seeds
- tomatoes
- turkey
- vanilla
- wild rice

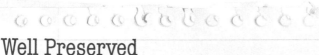

Well Preserved

The Incas were freeze-drying food in the Andes centuries before the US space program used freeze-drying for cosmic cuisine. Beef jerky is another clever method of food preservation contributed by American Indians. Pemmican, which was a preserved mixture of fat, lean meat, and sometimes dried berries, was enormously helpful to European explorers and traders, who carried it on expeditions to other continents.

US History: Who's the Boss?

Native Democracy

The Iroquois Confederacy, also known as the League of Peace and Power, was formed long before the Mayflower carried Pilgrims to North America. The nations of the Mohawk, Seneca, Oneida, Cayuga, Onondaga, and later the Tuscarora joined forces to end their own conflicts and became strong enough to defend themselves and attack others. That union shared an oral constitution called the Gayanashagowa, which was remembered by the leaders using a system of mnemonic beads.

When Benjamin Franklin was working on uniting the colonies, he culled from the model of the Iroquois Confederacy a system of government that had both central powers and particular powers reserved for states. Franklin also mined ideas about governing and individual rights from the many Indian treaties he printed in his printing-press business.

The States of US Rulers

Before Europeans arrived, the North American continent was filled with hundreds of sovereign nations and cultures with a variety of rulers, from tribal chiefs to shamans and councils. Before becoming part of the United States, the islands of Hawaii were ruled by monarchs, including a dynasty of five succeeding King Kamehamehas.

The thirteen colonies of mostly European settlers in North America first declared their independence from the King of Great Britain in 1776. Many battles later, victory induced a lot of head-scratching and debate to decide what to do with the hard-won freedom. By the late 1780s, a unique new constitution and system of government was developed.

States would have their own powers, but a president would be the head ruler for the whole country, serving as chief of the executive branch of a *federal* government and commander-in-chief of the armed forces. The president's power would not be absolute but complemented by a system of checks and balances that included a Congress of locally elected officials, and a court system to uphold the written Constitution.

George Washington became the first president of the United States in 1789, and in 2009, Barack Obama became the forty-fourth president of the United States. Obama is the forty-*third* man to serve as president, though. Grover Cleveland served as the twenty-second and twenty-fourth presidents, the only person to serve two non-consecutive terms. Presidential tenures have ranged from one month (William Henry Harrison) to twelve years (Franklin D. Roosevelt). Most were elected as president; others were vice presidents who took over when the president died in office.

The original thirteen colonies were the first sovereign states in the new nation's confederation in 1776. Those states ratified the new Constitution and joined the United States of America in the following order, from 1787 to 1790:

- Delaware
- Pennsylvania
- New Jersey
- Georgia
- Connecticut

- Massachusetts
- Maryland
- South Carolina
- New Hampshire
- Virginia

- New York
- North Carolina
- Rhode Island

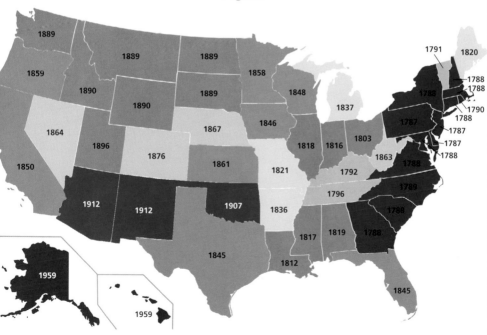

Here's the state of statehoods by date and color blocks.
The thirteen colonies are in red.

Presidential Statesmanship

Which president had the most states join the Union when he was in power?

Six states
BENJAMIN HARRISON (1889–1893)
North Dakota (1889)
South Dakota (1889)
Montana (1889)
Washington (1889)
Idaho (1890)
Wyoming (1890)

Five states
JAMES MONROE (1817–1825)
Mississippi (1817)
Illinois (1818)
Alabama (1819)
Maine (1820)
Missouri (1821)

Three states
GEORGE WASHINGTON (1789–1797)
Vermont (1791)
Kentucky (1792)
Tennessee (1796)

JAMES K. POLK (1845–1849)
Texas (1845)
Iowa (1846)
Wisconsin (1848)

JAMES BUCHANAN (1857–1861)
Minnesota (1858)
Oregon (1859)
Kansas (1861)

Two states
JAMES MADISON (1809–1817)
Louisiana (1812)
Indiana (1816)

ANDREW JACKSON (1829–1837)
Arkansas (1836)
Michigan (1837)

ABRAHAM LINCOLN (1861–1865)
West Virginia (1863)
Nevada (1864)

WILLIAM H. TAFT (1909–1913)
New Mexico (1912)
Arizona (1912)

DWIGHT D. EISENHOWER (1953–1961)
Alaska (1959)
Hawaii (1959)

One state
THOMAS JEFFERSON (1801–1809)
Ohio (1803)

JOHN TYLER (1841–1845)
Florida (1845)

MILLARD FILLMORE (1850–1853)
California (1850)

ANDREW JOHNSON (1865–1869)
Nebraska (1867)

ULYSSES S. GRANT (1869–1877)
Colorado (1876)

GROVER CLEVELAND (1893–1897)
Utah (1896)

THEODORE ROOSEVELT (1901–1909)
Oklahoma (1907)

Zero states
John Adams (1797–1801), John Q. Adams (1825–1829), Martin Van Buren (1837–1841), William H. Harrison (1841), Zachary Taylor (1849–1850), Franklin Pierce (1853–1857), Rutherford B. Hayes (1877–1881), James Garfield (1881), Chester A. Arthur (1881–1885), Grover Cleveland (1885–1889), William McKinley (1897–1901), Woodrow Wilson (1913–1921), Warren G. Harding (1921–1923), Calvin Coolidge (1923–1929), Herbert C. Hoover (1929–1933), Franklin D. Roosevelt (1933–1945), Harry S. Truman (1945–1953), John F. Kennedy (1961–1963), Lyndon B. Johnson (1963–1969), Richard M. Nixon (1969–1974), Gerald R. Ford, Jr. (1974–1977), James Carter, (1977–1981), Ronald W. Reagan (1981–1989), George H. W. Bush (1989–1993), William J. Clinton (1993–2001), George W. Bush (2001–2009), Barack Obama (2009–)

{ **fyi** }

At age forty-two, Teddy Roosevelt was the youngest person to become president. Ronald Reagan was the oldest president, taking office at age sixty-nine, just a few weeks before his seventieth birthday. James Garfield and John F. Kennedy were both in their forties when they were assassinated in office. John Adams, Herbert Hoover, Gerald Ford, and Ronald Reagan all lived into their nineties.

Dates to Remember

What do you think of when you hear the years 1492, 1776, and 1917? Do you know what else was going on in the world during that time?

1492

The year 1492 was a big one in American history. Columbus "sailed the ocean blue," trying to find a way to the spices and riches of the Indies—but he landed in the Bahamas. He even called the native inhabitants he encountered "Indians." Although he was later credited with discovering America, Columbus always thought he was in Asia, and he never actually set foot on the North American continent. Furthermore, archaeological evidence proves that the Vikings had settled the continent four centuries earlier, and many scholars argue that the Chinese got to North America long before Columbus tried to get to Asia. Columbus's arrival did trigger a massive movement of gold, silver, slaves, religions, and foods—as well as an age of "discovery" that dramatically changed the world by connecting the continents via sea voyages.

Meanwhile, back in Spain—the country that had financed Columbus's expedition—the Muslim Moors were forced out after Queen Isabella and King Ferdinand conquered Granada in 1492. Also that year, the rulers' Alhambra Decree ordered all Jews to convert to Catholicism or leave the Iberian peninsula. At least 150,000 Jews moved out to other parts of Europe,

North Africa, and Asia. The Moors and Jews had contributed greatly to the culture. Their expulsion created a real brain drain in Spain.

Later that decade, while Columbus continued to seek a Western route to the Spice Islands, John Cabot made a claim for Britain in North America, and Vasco da Gama headed south and east around Africa. Da Gama actually made it to the real India, where there were already a million non-white Christians, thanks to earlier groundwork laid by St. Thomas, one of the disciples of Jesus.

Babar, the Muslim founder of the Mughal Empire in India, was nine years old in 1492, absorbing the Persian influences that would change the mostly Hindu part of the world he would rule.

Although it was 1492 in other parts of the world, it was the year 7000 in Russia on a calendar that ended at the year 7000, the time when many Russians were expecting the apocalypse.

1776

The American colonies were not the only ones getting restless in 1776. A major Islamic revolution took place when Muslim Fulas in western Africa overthrew the Denanke Kingdom, a realm ruled by non-Muslims for several centuries. The Fulas created the Kingdom of Fouta Tooro in its place.

Spain created its last Vice Royalty in South America in 1776 to protect its power against the British and Portuguese. The Vice Royalty of the Río de la Plata included what are now Argentina, Paraguay, Uruguay, and Bolivia, as well as the widest river and estuary in the world, called "the Plate River" by the British.

Six years earlier, James Cooke and the English *Endeavour* crew charted the eastern coast of Australia, but it wasn't until 1788 that the first Europeans created a settlement—a penal colony.

In India, around twenty-five thousand people perished in the fight between the Jat and Rajput armies in one of the last huge battles under Jaipur rule prior to the British dominating the scene. It was known as the Battle of the Maonda and Manholdi. (For perspective, George Washington's army at the beginning of the American Revolution had only twenty thousand men.)

In Britain, Adam Smith's *Wealth of Nations* and Edward Gibbon's first volume of the *Rise and Fall of the Roman Empire* were both published in 1776, the year some people across the ocean drafted a Declaration of Independence.

1917

World War I was in its fourth deadly year. The Germans had launched a fierce submarine war. The US officially declared war on Germany on April 9 and provided critical manpower and aid to allies for victory. China and Greece also declared war against Germany. T. E. Lawrence and the Arabs were victorious against the Turks in Aqaba, Jordan. China's warlords were in conflict with Japan and with each other, and the Nationals and Communists began to struggle for control.

The Russian (or Bolshevik) Revolution of 1917 ended the Czarist rule of Russia, but did not bring peace and an end to Russia's involvement in World War I, as millions of peasants had hoped. A civil war followed, from 1918 to 1922, between the Red Army and White (anti-Communist) Russians.

Deaths from influenza and pneumonia were on the rise in 1917, building to a global pandemic by 1918. More than 40 million people were killed by this strain of the virus, which was particularly fatal for otherwise healthy young adults. About one third of the global population is estimated to have been infected.

World War I propaganda posters were prevalent in the US in 1917.

Extra Credit

Seven Ancient Wonders

There are many different kinds of "Seven Wonder" lists today. But, can you wonder backwards and name the seven wonders of the *ancient* world, when the first list was made?

Extra, extra credit if you know which wonder can still be visited, and which wonder inspired the word "mausoleum."

If you are wondering what the answers are, check page 137.

The Taj Mahal is <u>not</u> one of the seven wonders of the ancient world.

Literature & Grammar 101

WHO WROTE IN THE NUDE? WHAT DOES THE T. S. STAND FOR IN T. S. ELIOT? Which famous author with the first name of George is female? This chapter may arouse your curiosity about literary figures both great and grating, and you may even pick up some edifying grammar tips.

Are you one of those people who still has your favorite novels from college not far from a good dictionary and Strunk and White's *The Elements of Style*? Then you might not need an eccentric survey of literature and grammar, but you may want to know more about the quirks and quips of those beloved writers. Some memorable tips for even better writing couldn't hurt either.

Or are you someone who never wants to be reminded what iambic pentameter is, or what the scarlet letter stood for in Hawthorne's classic? Don't worry, that's not here. But who wouldn't want to be scintillating in any salon or saloon? Read on to add to your own cache of bon mots for future badinage, or just to shake your head and say, "Really?"

Genius at Work

Writers' positions in "literature" don't seem to be dependent on their position when writing. Whether the writer's tools are pen and paper, typewriters, computer keyboards, or touch screens, the creativity of a writer's body at work is as amusing as his or her body of work.

Outstanding "Stand Up" Writers

Not all writers sat at desks to craft their masterpieces. In the nineteenth century, it was not uncommon to write standing up, leaning on a lectern. There were also some upstanding writers (in posture if not always character) in the twentieth and twenty-first centuries.

One of the big guys of American literature in the twentieth century, Ernest Hemingway, said, "Writing and travel broaden your ass, if not your mind, and I like to write standing up."

One of the bright female stars of twentieth-century English literature, Virginia Woolf may have written standing up on occasion to treat her desk like an easel in emulation of (or rivalry with) her talented sister Vanessa, who painted.

Other literary luminaries rumored to stand as they wrote: Vladimir Nabokov, Lewis Carroll, and the very tall Thomas Wolfe. Philip Roth reportedly likes to pace between filling pages standing up.

Bed Writers

Mark Twain and Marcel Proust liked to write in bed. Truman Capote called himself a "horizontal author."

Naked Writers

As part of his health program, the author of *Poor Richard's Almanack*, Benjamin Franklin, enjoyed being naked and working with the windows open during his "air baths."

Literary Hotspots

Writing is usually a solitary occupation, but there have been times when creative clusters of writers, artists, and intellectuals in the same geographical area gathered and cross-pollinated, influencing each other and the larger literary world. There have also been specific places that, for a certain period, attracted creative people.

New England Transcendentalists

Active during the mid-nineteenth century (1830s–1850s), this group included writers who were also educators and philosophers, among them the essayist and poet Ralph Waldo Emerson and Henry David Thoreau, author of *Walden*. The transcendentalists aimed to shape an American voice and vision that was

Henry David Thoreau

independent of European literature. Nature, the human spirit, and divinity were topics often explored. The talented Margaret Fuller and Elizabeth Palmer Peabody helped publish the transcendentalist journal, *The Dial*. At Emerson's urging, Amos Bronson Alcott also moved to Concord, Massachusetts, and founded the Concord School of Philosophy. He encouraged his daughter, Louisa May Alcott (*Little Women*), to write. The work of New Englander Walt Whitman (*Leaves of Grass*) is often considered transcendental.

Louisa May Alcott

Algonquin Round Table

This literary Manhattan assemblage was known for its biting wit, as sharp as any sword. For about a decade (1919–1929), writers and editors gathered for weekday lunches at a particular table at the Algonquin Hotel in order to swap clever quips and jabs, as well as engage in lively conversation. Dorothy Parker (poet, short story writer, and screenwriter), Robert Benchley (humorist and actor), Alexander Wolcott (influential critic), Robert E. Sherwood (editor, playwright, and screenwriter), Heywood Broun (sports writer and humorist), and Harold Ross (*New Yorker* founder and editor) were all regular members. Friends of the table included Edna Ferber (playwright and novelist) and the silent Marx Brother, Harpo, who enjoyed talking off-screen with fellow wits. Away from the table, the creative gang loved to play croquet, cards, and practical jokes.

Bloomsbury Group

This refers to a group of artists, writers, and thinkers who gathered in the Bloomsbury part of London during the first decades of the twentieth century. Members of the nontraditional intellectual group influenced literature and economics and were generally known for advocating pacifism, gender equality, and sexual relations based on love, not monogamy. The Bloomsbury Group included Virginia Woolf (*A Room of One's Own*, *Mrs. Dalloway*, *To the Lighthouse*), Leonard Woolf (*Barbarians at the Gate*), E. M. Forster (*A Passage to India*), renowned economist John Maynard Keynes, literary critic Desmond MacCarthy, art critic Roger Fry, painter Duncan Grant, painter Vanessa Bell, and historian Lytton Strachey. Virginia and Leonard Woolf also founded Hogarth Press, which published the UK's first copies of T. S. Eliot's *The Waste Land*, translations of Freud, and pacifists' works.

Harlem Renaissance

Farther uptown from the Algonquin set, in Harlem, black writers, intellectuals, and artists were helping explore and shape a new pride, consciousness, and identity as African Americans during what became known as the Harlem Renaissance. Hundreds of thousands of black Americans left the rural South after World War I and migrated to northern urban centers. The three square miles of Harlem became a very concentrated and influential creative center during

Zora Neale Hurston

the 1920s and '30s. Langston Hughes (*Not Without Laughter*) and Zora Neale Hurston (*Their Eyes Were Watching God*) were two of the best-known writers. Other influential voices included Alain Locke (*The New Negro*), Arna Bontemps (*God Sends Sunday*), and Claude McKay (*Home to Harlem*).

Paris and Expats in the 1920s

After the First World War, American expatriates (expats) were part of a "Lost Generation" disillusioned by the war. They found each other in Paris, an epicenter for the Western arts. Magnets that drew them together in the City of Lights included Gertrude Stein's weekly salons and Sylvia Beach's bookstore, Shakespeare and Company, later revered for taking the risk of publishing James Joyce's *Ulysses*. Ernest Hemingway (*For Whom the Bell Tolls*, *The Sun Also Rises*) and F. Scott Fitzgerald (*The Great Gatsby*) were also improvising a new "American" prose in Jazz Age Paris.

Ernest Hemingway

Initially Great

Part of the literary quest involves exploring what characters represent, what the metaphors and symbols mean, and what whole is behind the fragments presented. With some authors you might also wonder, "What names are behind those initial initials?" (And in some cases, "What were their parents thinking?")

Pen Name	Birth Name	Claim to Fame
e. e. cummings	Edward Estlin Cummings	1958 Bollingen Prize, top poetry award
T. S. Eliot	Thomas Stearns Eliot	*The Love Song of J. Alfred Prufrock*, *The Waste Land*
E. M. Forster	Edward Morgan Forster	*A Room with a View*, *Howards End*, *A Passage to India*
D. H. Lawrence	David Herbert Richards Lawrence	*Women in Love*, *Lady Chatterly's Lover*
C. S. Lewis	Clive Staples Lewis	*The Chronicles of Narnia*, *The Space Trilogy*, *The Screwtape Letters*
H. P. Lovecraft	Howard Phillips Lovecraft	*The Call of Cthulhu*
J. K. Rowling	Joanne Rowling*	The Harry Potter series
J. D. Salinger	Jerome David Salinger	*The Catcher in the Rye*
J. R. R. Tolkien	John Ronald Reuel Tolkien	*The Hobbit*, *The Lord of the Rings*, *The Silmarillion*
W. B. Yeats	William Butler Yeats	1932 Nobel Prize in Literature for his poetry
H. G. Wells	Herbert George Wells	*The Time Machine*, *The War of the Worlds*
E. B. White	Elwyn Brooks White	*Charlotte's Web*, *Stuart Little*, *The Elements of Style*

*The "K" was a bow to her Aunt Kathleen, added when publishers asked her to form a gender-neutral pen name with two initials.

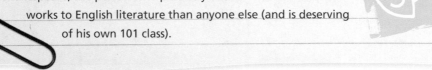

Keep Reading!

"I say there is no darkness, but ignorance," wrote William Shakespeare, the person who probably added more words and works to English literature than anyone else (and is deserving of his own 101 class).

The Gender Question

Eudora Welty, Ezra Pound, Flannery O'Connor, George Eliot, George Sand, and Harper Lee were all great writers, but were they male or female? See page 137 for the answers.

{ fyi }

Most lit lovers know the name Montaigne, but what's the rest of the name? The emergence of the essay as a literary form is credited to Michel Eyquem de Montaigne, an important figure in the French Renaissance. Although he was born into a wealthy family, the first several years of Montaigne's life were spent with peasants in a humble cottage. His humanist father wanted him to develop compassion for the poor and to know the people he could later help. As a small child, he was then brought to the family chateau, with servants who were instructed to speak only Latin, so he would learn the language. A zither player was always nearby for him to enjoy live music at any time.

Burn or Learn?

For as long as books have existed, the power of the printed word has stirred controversy and occasionally resulted in censorship. Books have been burned, banned, or "challenged" for their sexual content, profanity, violence, religious orientation, and political positions.

Nazi Book Burnings

In 1933, Nazi Germany staged public bonfires to purge the country of books with "anti-German" thinking. An estimated twenty-five thousand books were destroyed, including Ernest Hemingway's *The Sun Also Rises*, Jack London's *The Call of the Wild*, Upton Sinclair's *The Jungle*, and Theodore Dreiser's *An American Tragedy*. In 1946, at the end of WWII, the occupying Allied forces collected and destroyed at least as many books, including poetry and school books that were said to contribute to militarism or Nazism.

Banned Books

The last week of every September is declared Banned Books Week in the United States. Many libraries and academic organizations hold events then to examine our freedoms and celebrate literature. Here are a few classic books that were once banned:

Lolita, by Vladimir Nabokov, features a troubled middle-aged man and his sexual obsession with a twelve-year-old girl. The innovative novel was deemed "obscene" and banned in France, where it was first published in 1955. Nabokov later translated his work into Russian, but this did not make it any less controversial.

Adventures of Huckleberry Finn, by Mark Twain (a.k.a. Samuel Clemens), is often regarded as one of the great American novels. The sequel to *The Adventures of Tom Sawyer* is an odyssey down the Mississippi River taken by two characters seeking freedom—a runaway slave and a boy escaping an abusive father. Written in colorful, local vernacular, the sometimes-rough language has bothered some people who don't think it belongs in a school library. More recently, others have argued that the book perpetuates "racial stereotypes," and they object to the use of the n-word.

Fahrenheit 451, by Ray Bradbury, is a cautionary tale about what happens when people stop thinking. The title refers to the temperature at which books burn. The story includes the words "damn" and "hell," and in showing the dangers of book burning, it depicts a Bible and great works of literature being burned. Some found that offensive and, ironically, cause for *it* to be banned.

To Kill a Mockingbird, by Harper Lee, is a Pulitzer Prize–winning classic about learning tolerance in a racially prejudiced small Southern town during the Depression; but various libraries and schools were intolerant of the book. For decades, some educators have wanted this book banned because of its language (citing "damn," "whore," and the n-word, among others) and its portrayals of rape and racism.

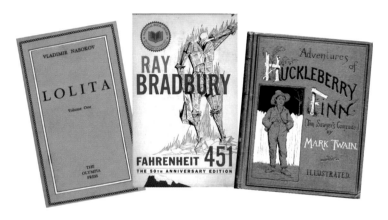

Lolita, *Fahrenheit 451*, and *Huckleberry Finn* were all banned at one point.

Enviable?

Jane Austen, one of England's finest writers, known for her irony, humor, and insight, lived before the literary prizes of Pulitzer, Nobel, and Booker. Still, the long-enduring popularity of her novels (*Pride and Prejudice, Sense and Sensibility,* and *Emma*) and their successful afterlife as Hollywood movies could be the envy of many writers and screenwriters. But beware: The Austen family coat of arms includes the Latin motto *"Qui invidit minor est,"* which roughly translates as "Whoever envies me is smaller than I."

Pulitzer Prize for Literature: Fiction

If you want to enjoy some award winning reads, these books all won the Pulitzer Prize for Fiction. Bestowed since 1948, the honor goes to an American author for a great work of literature, usually one that explores American life.

2010	*Tinkers,* by Paul Harding
2009	*Olive Kitteridge,* by Elizabeth Strout
2008	*The Brief Wondrous Life of Oscar Wao,* by Junot Diaz
2007	*The Road,* by Cormac McCarthy
2006	*March,* by Geraldine Brooks
2005	*Gilead,* by Marilynne Robinson
2004	*The Known World,* by Edward P. Jones
2003	*Middlesex,* by Jeffrey Eugenides
2002	*Empire Falls,* by Richard Russo
2001	*The Amazing Adventures of Kavalier & Clay,* by Michael Chabon
2000	*Interpreter of Maladies,* by Jhumpa Lahiri
1999	*The Hours,* by Michael Cunningham
1998	*American Pastoral,* by Philip Roth
1997	*Martin Dressler: The Tale of an American Dreamer,* by Steven Millhauser
1996	*Independence Day,* by Richard Ford
1995	*The Stone Diaries,* by Carol Shields
1994	*The Shipping News,* by E. Annie Proulx
1993	*A Good Scent from a Strange Mountain,* by Robert Olen Butler
1992	*A Thousand Acres,* by Jane Smiley
1991	*Rabbit at Rest,* by John Updike
1990	*The Mambo Kings Play Songs of Love,* by Oscar Hijuelos
1989	*Breathing Lessons*, by Anne Tyler
1988	*Beloved*, by Toni Morrison
1987	*A Summons to Memphis*, by Peter Taylor
1986	*Lonesome Dove*, by Larry McMurtry
1985	*Foreign Affairs*, by Alison Lurie
1984	*Ironweed*, by William Kennedy
1983	*The Color Purple*, by Alice Walker
1982	*Rabbit Is Rich*, by John Updike
1981	*A Confederacy of Dunces*, by the late John Kennedy Toole (a posthumous publication)

continued on next page

Pulitzer Prize for Literature: Fiction (continued)

1980   *The Executioner's Song*, by Norman Mailer
1979   *The Stories of John Cheever*, by John Cheever
1978   *Elbow Room*, by James Alan McPherson
1977   (No Award)
1976   *Humboldt's Gift*, by Saul Bellow
1975   *The Killer Angels*, by Michael Shaara
1974   (No Award)
1973   *The Optimist's Daughter*, by Eudora Welty
1972   *Angle of Repose*, by Wallace Stegner
1971   (No Award)
1970   *Collected Stories*, by Jean Stafford
1969   *House Made of Dawn*, by N. Scott Momaday
1968   *The Confessions of Nat Turner*, by William Styron
1967   *The Fixer*, by Bernard Malamud
1966   *Collected Stories*, by Katherine Anne Porter

1965   *The Keepers of the House*, by Shirley Ann Grau
1964   (No Award)
1963   *The Reivers*, by William Faulkner
1962   *The Edge of Sadness*, by Edwin O'Connor
1961   *To Kill a Mockingbird*, by Harper Lee
1960   *Advise and Consent*, by Allen Drury
1959   *The Travels of Jaimie McPheeters*, by Robert Lewis Taylor
1958   *A Death in the Family*, by the late James Agee
       (a posthumous publication)
1957   (No Award)
1956   *Andersonville*, by MacKinlay Kantor
1955   *A Fable*, by William Faulkner
1954   (No Award)
1953   *The Old Man and the Sea*, by Ernest Hemingway
1952   *The Caine Mutiny*, by Herman Wouk

1951   *The Town*, by Conrad Richter
1950   *The Way West*, by A. B. Guthrie
1949   *Guard of Honor*, by James Gould Cozzens
1948   *Tales of the South Pacific*, by James A. Michener

Spell Check

Several famous people have been credited with saying something like, "It's a dull man who can only spell a word one way," yet creative spelling is generally not appreciated. To complicate things, although there are rules like "*i* before *e* except after *c*," our **species** has found that such a **weird** rule is not **sufficient**, since it does not apply to **science**, **conscience**, or **leisure**.

Smart Spelling

Spell-check programs and text messaging may change the future of spelling, but for now there is usually only one accepted way to spell a word in American English. Sometimes that spelling seems capricious and arbitrary, but if you put the right letters in the right order, people tend to think you are better educated. When you see a misspelled word, does it disturb you or make you feel knowledgeable?

> *If you are embarassed by mispelling words, then you might want to exersice good judgement and acknowlege, without argumant, that you should be dependant on the existance of a dictionary and make a committment to look up words, weather you do it on occassion or its a regular occurence. Of coarse, if you are writing on a computer, its a seperate issue and you have the privelege and perogative to use a program to check you're spelling before you preceed to printing, to insure that you haven't inadvertantly misspelled anything.*

What's wrong with the above paragraph? If you found twenty words that are spelled wrong, and you know how to spell them correctly (see page 38), you deserve a vacation.

And don't forget to take a pole, maybe you can catch a *ghoti*. "Ghoti" is how you would spell "fish," if you took the *f*-sounding "gh" from the word *tough,* the *i*-sounding "o" from *women* (wimin), and the *sh*-sounding "ti" from *nation.* The word "ghoti" has been used for over a hundred years as an example of the erratic nature of English spelling and the need for consistency between letters and their sounds.

Twenty words spelled correctly:

1) *embarrassed*
2) *misspelling*
3) *exercise*
4) *judgment*
5) *acknowledge*
6) *argument*
7) *dependent*
8) *existence*
9) *commitment*
10) *whether ("weather" is part of the climate)*
11) *occasion*
12) *it's ("it's" is the contraction of "it is")*
13) *occurrence*
14) *course ("coarse" is the opposite of "fine")*
15) *separate*
16) *privilege*
17) *prerogative*
18) *your ("you're" is the contraction of "you are")*
19) *proceed*
20) *inadvertently*

Are You Able to Ible?

How can you remember which is which and why?

Well, if the root word is *in*complete, like "incred-" or "poss-," you add "-ible" to make it po*ssible* to be incred*ible*.

You add "-able" to the end if the root word is complete (like "fashion" or "depend") to be depend*able* and fashion*able*.

Still, wanting to cover everything, you may recall that there are some *irritable* and *contemptible* exceptions to these rules, so it's *inevitable* that, as with other parts of English grammar, you need to stay *flexible* to be *responsible*.

{ fyi }

George Bernard Shaw was the only writer to get both a Nobel Prize for Literature and an Oscar. The haphazardness of English spelling bothered him so much that he willed part of his estate to be used to create an alphabet that would allow words to be spelled like they sound. Royalties from Shaw's *Pygmalion* and the movie *My Fair Lady*, based on *Pygmalion*, helped fund the "Shavian alphabet" after his death.

This new system has not been widely adopted, though, so writers who aspire for their own Oscars or Nobel Prizes still need to learn about spelling and grammar.

Grappling with Grammar

Grammar is a set of guidelines to standardize our rebellious language that evolved from so many other languages. Every rule seems to have its rule-breakers, but the reminders below will work in most cases.

When Should I Say It's All About Me?

I am the subject of sentences. You can give objects to *me*. When you add other people into the mix, the rules stay the same.

> Horatio and *I* went to the planetarium.
>> NOT
> Horatio and *me* saw stars. (You wouldn't say "Me saw stars," unless you were a cosmic Tarzan.)
> Aunt Maggie gave Chris and *me* her flutes.
>> NOT
> Aunt Maggie gave Chris and *I* her flutes. (You wouldn't say "She gave *I* a piano.")

In other words, even in our self-centered culture, "Me say, it's all about I" is wrong, because "I say, it's all about me."

Do You *Lie* or *Lay*?

Forget for a moment issues of deceit and truth and that kind of *lie,* or what you tried to do for a good *lay* in college.

If you simply want to get horizontal on the couch, the rules of *lay* and *lie* could incite a headache, or suddenly make you think that you really just want to nap or sleep sitting up.

When you wake up, the general rules will still be: You *lie* down, and you *lay* something else down or on, if you are speaking in the present. If you are talking about the past, you *lay* down and you *laid* something else down or on.

Now that we have *laid* this on you (past tense), you can go *lie* down in the present. Sweet dreams.

They're There at *Their* House

They're, *there*, and *their* are homophones. (Relax, it just means they sound the same.) But *they're, there,* and *their* each have a different meaning and function.

They're is the contraction of *they are*, and contains a verb. Whenever you mean "they are," *they're* is the winner.

There is an adverb, usually a place or an idea: "There are Martians who walked there."

If you want to modify something and show who possesses it, then *their* is your word. Use *their* like you would use *our*. If you like mnemonic devices (memory tips), note that both *our* and *their* have two vowels in a row and show plural possession.

If you can substitute *our* in the sentence and it makes sense, then you want *their*. You wouldn't write "Our there at their house" or "They're our at their house," because "They're there at our house." Wonder how they got there?

It's About *Its*

Misusing *it's* and *its* is one of the most common mistakes in this finger-flying keyboard world. If you see the word *it's*, think to yourself *it is*. *It's* is a contraction, like "*There's* nothing to do," not a possessive like "the tree and *its* long branches."

So, it's (as in *it is*) not correct to write, "*Its* going to rain," or "I love the house; *it's* (it is) walls are tall." Please repeat after all grammarians: "*It's* stands for *it is*.'"

You're Your Best Friend

Can you now ace when to use *your* or *you're*? It's that contraction thing they're always wanting us to learn. *You're* stands for *you are. Your* is possessive—as in "your house, your rules."

When in Doubt, Break It Out

it's = it is
they're = they are
you're = you are

The words its, their, there, and your do not have verbs.

Because You Use Since Incorrectly...

It's not really correct to say, "Since earthquakes wreak havoc, I am moving." *Since* refers to time, not causal reasons: "You have loved pizza since you were five years old." Use *because* if you want to link consequences: "Because you are funny, people laugh."

Over and More Than

Over, like *above* and *under,* refers to a physical position, a spatial reference, such as "The Frisbee flew over his car." *Over* wasn't intended to describe an amount. Use of language changes though, and in conversation and idiomatic writing it's considered okay now to say, "He has over twenty books in his library" or "Over a century ago. . ." If you want to write properly though, remember:

More than means *additional.* "I have more than a trillion dollars" would be proper usage (and a nice fantasy).

Extra credit

Word Wisdom

Now that you're a spelling and grammar pro and have improved your literature expertise, it's time to enhance your vocabulary. Whether you want to be omniscient, perspicacious, or sentient, it helps to have a good vocabulary if you want to at least *sound* like you know everything. Try matching the words on the left with their definitions on the right. Bonus extra credit if you figure out which noun describes an act that contributed to two wars in Prague.

1. afflatus
2. cabalistic
3. defenestration
4. onomatopoeia
5. philomath
6. polymath
7. prospicience
8. pulchritudinous
9. senectitude
10. sibylline

A. *(n) old age; the last stage of life; elder phase of life*

B. *(n) intelligent and learned in many areas of knowledge*

C. *(n) the act of looking forward, knowing in advance*

D. *(adj) physically beautiful, attractive*

E. *(adj) hidden, secret meanings*

F. *(n) name-making; when a word sounds like what it describes, such as buzz or quack*

G. *(adj) prophetic*

H. *(n) sudden divine inspiration or knowledge*

I. *(n) a lover of learning*

J. *(n) the act of being thrown out a window*

Please do not try defenestration before (or after) you seek confirmation of your correct answers on page 138.

Math 101

WAIT! THIS IS NOT WHAT YOU THINK—DON'T TURN TO ANOTHER CHAPTER yet. Stories about love, homicide, cults, and intrigue lurk here, as well as references to *The Simpsons*, Renaissance painting, and gambling, and even tales of how math has saved lives.

Math is your friend, not your nemesis. Don't be scared if you don't remember what a quadratic equation is, or if the only pi (π) you want is edible. From the beginning, math was developed to make life easier, better, more beautiful, and safer—whether providing a way to tell a fellow cave person how many beasts were out there, or triangulating satellite signals so your cell phone works.

Math is a tool of both business and science. It serves the practical commerce of daily life, but is also one of humanity's most exquisite vehicles for comprehending the invisible. Mathematical thinking can transform the abstract to the concrete, and the concrete to the abstract.

Many great minds through the centuries have used mathematical thinking in business, law, science, philosophy, and invention. The outstanding early philosophers, Socrates, Aristotle, Thales, and Pythagoras, were all mathematicians, trying to figure out how the world works.

Today, too, finding solutions for life's unknown variables (sometimes called *x* and *y*) goes far beyond a textbook exercise. So this chapter won't have you sharpening your pencil to do calculations, but it could sharpen your mind. And you might laugh, too.

Intriguing Mathematicians

Erase all images you have of mathematicians as risk-averse, quiet, boring types. Great mathematicians have led some of the most interesting lives in history.

Pythagoras

Pythagoras, who lived about 2,600 years ago, is best known for proving what is now called the Pythagorean theorem, although the Sumerians and Babylonians may have figured it out a lot earlier. Pythagoras founded a secretive religion based on the idea that numbers were the ultimate reality. Both women and men could join, and the inner circle was called the mathematikoi (sometimes translated as "those who study all"). Followers of his cult were also called geometers. Some say they swore to keep their work secret, and the violation of that oath was punishable by death.

The four triangles each have an area of six square units (half of a rectangle with 12 squares), and the center square has an area of one for a total area of 25 square units, so c must be 5 units. And we know a is 3 and b is 4 so $a^2 + b^2 = c^2$.

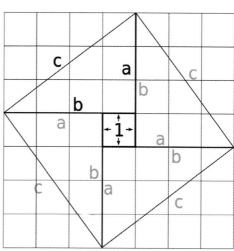

Pierre de Fermat

He lived more than four hundred years ago and was an attorney who did math in his spare time, taunting professional mathematicians with the proofs he was able to accomplish. His "amateur" work contributed to major branches of math that developed later, such as calculus, analytic geometry, number theory, and probability. He even continued provoking others from beyond the grave. A note found after his death in the margin of a book alluded to a "truly remarkable" proof he said he had completed, but the actual proof was never found. That was in 1630, and mathematicians spent the next several hundred years trying to prove "Fermat's Last Theorem." Finally, in 1994, British mathematician Andrew Wile developed an acceptable proof for Fermat's challenge from the seventeenth century. Interestingly, Wile relied on mathematical methods that didn't even exist until the twentieth century.

Évariste Galois (1811–1832)

A young political hothead and romantic during the time of the French Revolution, he challenged a man to a duel over a woman. Or, as some historians ask, was he deliberately goaded and set up for a dramatic end to his troublemaking? In anticipation of what Galois supposed would be his impending death, he spent the night before the duel writing out pages and pages of his mathematical ideas. He also kept repeatedly noting, "I have not time." Unfortunately, he was right: He walked his paces with his pistol and lost, dying the next day at age twenty. The insights contained in his scribblings were even more original and daring than his short life, and mathematicians spent years culling what they could. Some of the innovations were named after him, like the Galois field. Galois's approach to the algebra problems he studied has helped mathematicians in other fields as well, extending the impact of his last night's efforts and leaving people to wonder: What might Galois have achieved if he had failed to show up for that early-morning gunfight? (And what ever happened to the woman?)

Countess of Lovelace (1815–1852)

A memorable mathematician with a colorful life, she was the only legitimate daughter of poet Lord Byron (who called his wife the "Princess of Parallelograms"). Part of their daughter's prowess with numbers was applied (unsuccessfully) to creating a better betting system on horse races to alleviate her debts from her many wagers. She is often credited with inventing the first computer program, even though it was written for a computer that

Countess of Lovelace

hadn't been built yet. Not your typical married woman in the nineteenth century, Lady Lovelace foresaw that symbols and music, as well as digits, could serve as the language of machines. She was born as Augusta Ada Byron, and the computer programming language Ada was named after her.

Gregory Perelman (1966–)

Also called Grigori or Grisha, he is a modern-day Russian mathematical genius who solved one of the most challenging math problems of the twentieth century, a topology proof called the Poincaré Conjecture. Instead of writing up his work for professional journals, he posted his insights and solutions on the Internet. In 2006, he was chosen to receive the Fields Medal, the mathematics equivalent of the Nobel Prize. He not only turned down the honor, but he also refused to publish his works the traditional way, which would have qualified him for a different one-million-dollar prize. Perelman is rumored to live as a recluse with his mother in St. Petersburg to avoid the politics of math and the trappings of being a celebrity. He previously spent time teaching at top American universities, but now apparently prefers mushroom hunting.

Surprising Mathematicians

President James A. Garfield (1831–1881)

He created a new proof for the Pythagorean theorem while serving as a congressmen in 1876. He had intended to teach math in Ohio, but the Civil War changed the direction of his life. As president, he had fervent plans for educational reform, but was assassinated in 1881, just a few months after taking the office.

$$a^2 + b^2 = c^2$$

Garfield's proof of the Pythagorean theorem involves finding the area of the trapezoid containing two identical right triangles and half a square.

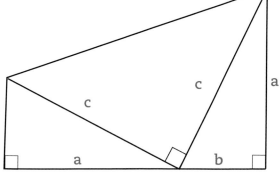

Danica McKellar (1975–)

A contemporary actress who starred as Winnie in the television series *The Wonder Years* (1988–1993), she received her mathematics degree from UCLA in 1998. While there, she coauthored the Chayes-McKellar-Winn theorem in a paper titled "Percolation and Gibbs States Multiplicity for Ferromagnetic Ashkin-Teller Models on $\mathbf{Z}^2$," which gives you an idea of the complexity of the topic. She's also written two popular books—*Math Doesn't Suck* and *Kiss My Math*—designed to help teen and preteen girls understand the wonders of math.

Florence Nightingale (1820–1910)

"The Lady with the Lamp," who created modern nursing during the Crimean Wars, applied statistics and unique graphics to change social policy and create medical practices that saved thousands of lives. She gathered data from hospitals in the war zone and realized that sanitation problems were a greater killer than war and the original diseases that brought people to the hospitals. Her insights helped convince both the royalty and military to improve the situation, and her work changed the way people looked at medical practice.

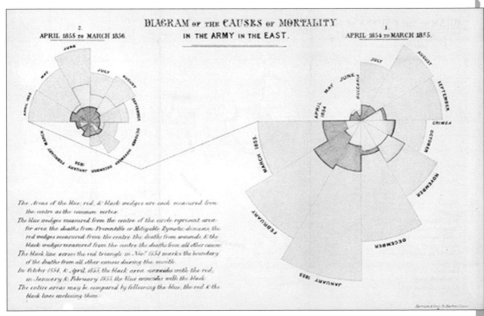

Diagram of the Causes of Mortality, by Florence Nightingale.

René Descartes (1596–1650)

The seminal philosopher who uttered "*Cogito ergo sum*" ("I think, therefore I am") was also the pivotal mathematician in the seventeenth century who figured out how to apply algebra to show geometry. He used the graphing system now named for him (the Cartesian plane), a vital precursor to calculus. He also started the use of superscripts to express exponents, as in the ^{2} in 10^2 for 10 times 10. (See the Power of Ten, page 52.)

TV writers

Several writers from the animated television series *The Simpsons* hold advanced degrees in math from top universities, and the comedy series is embedded with math jokes. J. Stewart Burns wrote about algebra for his master's degree from Harvard before he wrote humor for the series. Ken Keeler received a PhD from Harvard in applied mathematics before getting Homer and Bart in and out of trouble. Al Jean, the executive producer and head writer, graduated cum laude from Harvard with a BS in math. *D'oh* to the nth degree!

We've Got Your Number

Natural Numbers are the ones you can count naturally on your hands. It would not be natural to count a fraction of a finger or negative fingers. So, for example, both 42 and 1,000,000 are natural numbers (even if it is a lot of finger counting!).

$$1 \quad 2 \quad 3 \quad 4 \quad 5 \quad 6 \quad 7 \quad 8 \quad 9 \quad 10 \quad 11 \quad 12 \quad 13 \ldots$$

Whole Numbers include zero plus the natural numbers. If that big round O in whOle makes you think of zerO, you might remember it better. It also makes sense that whole numbers wouldn't be negative or cut up in parts like fractions.

$$0 \quad 1 \quad 2 \quad 3 \quad 4 \quad 5 \quad 6 \quad 7 \quad 8 \quad 9 \quad 10 \quad 11 \quad 12 \ldots$$

Integers are whole numbers and their opposites. The opposite of a positive number is the same number, only negative. The opposite of a positive two is negative two—they are both equidistant from the zero on a number line (see below).

$$\ldots -5 \quad -4 \quad -3 \quad -2 \quad -1 \quad 0 \quad 1 \quad 2 \quad 3 \quad 4 \quad 5 \ldots$$

Number Lines

Remember number lines? All the numbers are ordered with bigger numbers to the right of smaller numbers. Zero usually appears in the middle. All the numbers to the right of zero are positive, and all the numbers to the left are negative. And though the numbers to the left of zero may look like they are getting bigger (if you don't consider the negative sign), they are actually getting smaller *because* of the negative sign. Here's one way to look at it: If you owe somebody $200 (–200), your net worth is less than if you only owed $100 (–100), so –200 should go to the left of –100.

Negative Numbers are not numbers that have an attitude problem. They are the *opposite* of positive numbers—this includes natural numbers (see previous page) and rational and imaginary numbers (see below). The number without the sign on either side of zero represents its distance from zero and is called the *absolute value*. The absolute values of a number and of its opposite are the same. The sign represents the direction: + is to the right, – is to the left. When you add a number and its opposite, you get zero.

$$\ldots\ -14\ \ -13\ \ -12\ \ -11\ \ -10\ \ -9\ \ -8\ \ -7\ \ldots$$

Rational numbers may seem to be a contradiction in terms to those intimidated by math, especially by fractions, but the term does not refer to a state of mind. *Rational* comes from *ratio*, and *rational numbers* include all the integers (the whole numbers and their opposites) and the fractions in between, because they are all ratios. If there is only one guy available for every two gals, there is a 1-to-2 ratio. A ratio of one male to two females could be written as one over two, or $\frac{1}{2}$, which would express that there are only half as many guys as there are gals. A ratio of 2-to-1 would express that there are two gals for every guy, and $\frac{2}{1}$, or 2, would express that there are twice as many women. These ratios describe the same situation differently, and if you want to sound really smart, you can refer to them as *reciprocal ratios*. Whether you are a guy or a gal, that may or may not seem rational, but it is a ratio!

$$\ldots\ -1\ -\tfrac{3}{4}\ -\tfrac{1}{2}\ -\tfrac{1}{4}\ -\tfrac{1}{8}\ \ 0\ \ \tfrac{1}{8}\ \ \tfrac{1}{4}\ \ \tfrac{1}{2}\ \ \tfrac{3}{4}\ \ 1\ \ldots$$

Irrational numbers are numbers that can't be expressed as a nice, neat ratio of one integer to another to make a fraction. The best-known irrational number is probably the ratio of the distance around a circle (circumference) to the widest width of the circle (the diameter). That ratio is always the same number, which has been given the name *pi*. It is written as π, because you can't write it as a fraction. If you write it as a decimal, it comes out to 3.14159 . . . and then goes on and on and on infinitely without any repeating sequence, using a string of numbers that would go from here to the moon and beyond. Does that seem like a rational number? It's not. In fact, another equally good definition of *irrational number* is "any decimal that goes on forever without repeating."

$$\pi = 3.141592653589793238462643383279502884197169399375105820974944 5...$$

Imaginary numbers help mathematicians describe things that live only in their imaginations. What is the length of a side of a square with an area of −1? Let's face it. That's a silly question! Squares like that don't exist! That's why mathematicians had to *imagine* the number *i*, which is equal to the square root of negative one.

$$i = \sqrt{-1}$$

Prime numbers belong to an exclusive club. A prime number can only be divided by two numbers: itself and 1. For example, 40 can be divided evenly by 5 and by 2 (as well as other numbers), so 40 is not prime. But 41? There are no other integers besides one and forty-one that divide evenly into 41, so it's prime!

Prime of Life

Are you in the prime of life? Well, how old are you? If you are 2, 3, 5, 7, 11, 13, 17, 19, 23, 29, 31, 37, 41, 43, 47, 53, 59, 61, 67, 71, 73, 79, 83, 89, 97, 101, 103, 107, or 109 years old, you could say you are in "the prime of life."

The Power of Ten

Ten times ten (10^2) is one hundred. But with countless galaxies and trillion-dollar budgets these days, one hundred doesn't get you very far. Here are the names of some of the other powers of ten.

10^{18} or 1,000,000,000,000,000,000   one quintillion
10^{15} or 1,000,000,000,000,000   one quadrillion
10^{12} or 1,000,000,000,000   one trillion
10^{9} or 1,000,000,000   one billion
10^{6} or 1,000,000   one million
10^{3} or 1,000   one thousand
10^{2} or 100   one hundred
10^{1} or 10   ten
10^{0} or 1   one
10^{-1} or 0.1   one-tenth
10^{-2} or 0.01   one-hundredth
10^{-3} or 0.001   one-thousandth
10^{-6} or 0.000001   one-millionth
10^{-9} or 0.000000001   one-billionth
10^{-12} or 0.000000000001   one-trillionth
10^{-15} or 0.000000000000001   one-quadrillionth
10^{-18} or 0.000000000000000001   one-quintillionth

If you are feeling very powerful, you may want to know that 10^{21} is a sextillion, 10^{30} is a nonillion, 10^{39} is a dodecillion, 10^{63} is a vigitillion, and 10^{9999} is one tremilliatrecendotrigintillion.

{ fyi }

Although the numbers have no mathematical significance, mathematicians call 10^{100} a "googol," and 10^{googol} is a "googolplex."

So Many Branches, So Little Time

Algebra, statistics, and calculus, oh my! There are dozens of different types of math to sink your teeth into, but let's start with some of the basics.

Y Algebra?

• Clay tablets in cuneiform from the Babylonians, dating from around 1800 to 1600 BCE, include math that covers fractions, some algebra, and quadratic equations. That's almost four thousand years ago!

$$3x + 2y = 31 \quad y = 5$$
$$\text{What's } x?$$

• The word algebra comes from an Arabic word meaning "reunion" that was part of the title of a book written in 820 CE by Muhammad ibn Musa al-Khwarizmi. The book included some recipes, or algorithms, for solving certain math problems.

• Algebra today is the branch of math that includes understanding the operations of numbers (multiplication, subtraction, etc.) and the ability to work with symbols and sets of elements. Polynomials and factorization are also basic parts of algebra.

• Algebra often requires solving for the unknown, represented by x and y. It includes balancing equations using given information to solve problems. (Sounds like life, doesn't it?)

• Algebra is used every day in commerce, science, and engineering. Most people do algebra daily without even realizing it. If there are four of you at dinner, for example, and a pizza arrives with eight pieces, you might deduce that each person can have two slices. You've just done algebra (and showed what a fair person you are, not claiming three pieces as a reward for your mathematical abilities)!

Mary Somerville, born in 1780, became fascinated with algebra as a teenager, but her father was afraid its mental requirements would drive any woman insane. She memorized Euclid's geometry books by day and worked on problems at night in her head, while her family thought she was sleeping. She went on to become one of the greatest female scientists of the nineteenth century. She published her fourth science book at the age of 89.

Geometrically Cool

• *Geometry,* or "earth measure" in Greek, is one of the oldest and most practical sciences. It is the art and science, as well as theory and application, of the measurement of shapes and their places in space.

• Thales of Miletus used geometry to measure the distance of ships and the height of pyramids over 2,500 years ago. The story goes that he waited until his shadow was the same as his height and measured the shadow of the pyramid. He used that information to then calculate the distance from the edge of the pyramid to the center to help determine its true height.

• Geometry is based largely on a handful of concepts that we accept without proof, what mathematicians call *axioms*. The axioms are the foundation of all further geometric thinking and are used to "prove" solutions and theorems.

• Around 300 BCE, Euclid wrote *The Elements*, which has become one of the most significant, long-lasting textbooks ever created. *The Elements* clearly presented axioms, theorems, and proofs, some of which were previously known and some of which Euclid created. It forms the basis of Euclidean geometry, and was seminal in the development of logic and science through the centuries.

• Non-Euclidean geometry offers an alternative to Euclid's fifth postulate, which considers the existence of parallel lines. Specifically, in Euclidean geometry, if you have a straight line on a piece of paper (a flat plane) and you have a point, there is only *one* line you can draw through the point that will *not* intersect with the first line. But what if *lines* are more like the longitude grids on a globe? Don't those "parallel" lines meet at the poles?

• In non-Euclidian geometry (like elliptical or hyperbolic geometry), a straight line might not be the shortest distance between two points. There may be an infinite number of equally direct ways to get from point A to point B. This is a space- and mind-bender that is enjoyed in science fiction and twentieth-century science. Einstein used both Euclidean and non-Euclidean geometry for his breakthroughs.

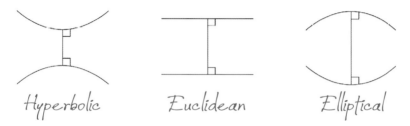

Hyperbolic   Euclidean   Elliptical

In each of these three kinds of geometric space, the horizontal lines are considered "straight"—not unlike the way the lines of latitude on a globe are straight.

Tips on Trig

Trigonometry, which is Greek for "triangle measure," may not seem like something you need every day, but triangulation gives us cell phone service, GPS, and satellite television. Trigonometry (or Trig) is used in navigation, astronomy, and oceanography, and is the framework for a whole lot more. You could say it provides the sines (pronounced "signs") of our times that keep much of technology going.

Explore the tips and trigonometric equations and definitions on the next page, and you might find some very cool relationships (without having to commit to anything on the first date).

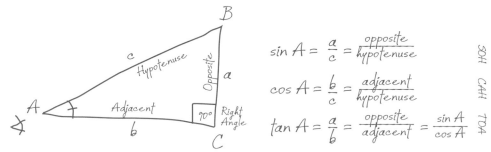

$$\sin A = \frac{a}{c} = \frac{opposite}{hypotenuse}$$

$$\cos A = \frac{b}{c} = \frac{adjacent}{hypotenuse}$$

$$\tan A = \frac{a}{b} = \frac{opposite}{adjacent} = \frac{\sin A}{\cos A}$$

SOH   CAH   TOA

If you know the measurements of one side and one angle of a right triangle, you can figure out the other angles and distances with the formulae of trigonometry, providing a method for indirect measurement. This helps people in architecture, navigation, astronomy, optics, chemistry, and many more fields.

Math Meets Life: Consider This

- The next time you are in a coffee shop, consider this: A doughnut and a coffee mug are the same shape—to topologists. **Topology** means "place study" in Greek and concerns what happens to surfaces and shapes when they are stretched without tearing. Because they both have only one hole, a doughnut (with its hole in the center) and a coffee mug (with its hole through the handle) are considered to have the same basic shape. (That round surface you sip from on your mug may look like a hole to you, but it is a continuous part of the mug, not a portal to see through, like the hole in the handle.) If your waitress is a topologist, make sure she doesn't pour your coffee on the doughnut. Come to think of it, if you are a topologist, remember not to bite into the coffee cup!

- The next time you see a child counting on ten fingers (a.k.a. digits), consider this: For all their complexity, computers can only use two digits for their calculations, but they can do it very fast. All data in computers— sounds, words, numbers, and images—are expressed in the form of a combination of ones and zeros. It's called the **binary system**.

- The next time you want to figure out the odds for gambling, consider this: A question about winnings sparked an exchange of letters between Blaise Pascal and Pierre de Fermat in 1654. The issue was how to split the pot of money being gambled when two men stopped playing a game before they were finished. The Pascal-Fermat correspondence yielded the beginning of **probability** as a discipline of math.

- The next time you enjoy a beautiful Renaissance painting, consider this: Until 1413, when painters started using **geometric perspective** to create vanishing points, most paintings were very flat and two-dimensional, with no way to convey depth on the canvas.

Lamentation (The Mourning of Christ) by Giotto di Bondone (1266–1337), at left, is flat and does not use geometric perspective. However, Pietro Perugino's (1446–1524) fresco in the Sistine Chapel (*Christ Handing the Keys to St. Peter*, 1481–2), at right, uses perspective to create a vanishing point, which was a painting method that only first appeared in Renaissance works.

Are You Ready to Convert?

How do you convert yards to feet? Multiply the number of yards by three. How do you convert feet to inches? Multiply the number of feet by twelve (because there are twelve inches in a foot).

But those are the *easy* non-metric conversions. If you want to be more knowledgeable and worldly, you might want to brush up on other units of measurement, too.

Suppose somebody tells you how many knots her boat goes. Or your hotel clerk in Europe tells you it's 30 degrees outside—in centigrade. Or maybe you want to bet on a horse race that is so many furlongs, and the horse you think has a rockin' name is so-many hands high. What does it all mean? How can you convert those into "real" measurements?

The charts on the next page will help. And to celebrate, we'll even let you know how many gallons are in a barrel of beer, or a barrel of gas, if you prefer.

Conversions

Ready to convert further? To make the conversions below, multiply the first terms by the multiplier to get the second terms.

To Convert From	To	Multiplier
AT SEA		
knots (nautical mi/hr)	kilometers/hour	1.852
knots (nautical mi/hr)	statute miles/hour	1.151
fathoms	feet	6
fathoms	meters	1.8288
nautical leagues	nautical miles	3
statute leagues	kilometers	4.828032
nautical miles	statute miles	1.1507794
RACY STUFF		
furlongs	feet	660
furlongs	meters	201.168
furlongs	statute miles	0.125
hands (height of horse)	centimeters	10.16
hands (height of horse)	inches	4
DRINK UP		
US beer barrels	gallons	31
US beer barrels	liters	117.34777
cups	liquid ounces (US)	8
cups	liters	0.2365882
liquid ounces (US)	liquid drams	8
liquid ounces (US)	liquid ounces (British)	1.041
liquid ounces (US)	liquid quarts	0.03125
GAS UP		
US petroleum barrels	gallons (British)	34.97
US petroleum barrels	gallons (US)	42

To Convert From	To	Multiplier
SURVEY THE LAND		
acres	square feet	43,560
acres	square meters	4,046.8564224
acres	square miles (statute)	0.00156250
square kilometers	statute miles	0.38610216
GOING METRIC		
centimeters	inches	0.3937008
inches	centimeters	2.54
inches	meters	0.0254
feet	centimeters	30.48
centimeters	feet	0.03280840
centimeters	meters	0.01
centimeters	yards	0.01093613
cubic centimeters	cubic inches	0.061023744
meters	centimeters	100
meters	feet	3.280839895
meters	inches	39.370079
meters	kilometers	0.001
meters	millimeters	1,000
kilometers	meters	1,000
kilograms	metric tons	0.001
kilograms	troy pounds	2.679229
kilometers	statute miles	0.621371192
square kilometers	acres	247.10538
square kilometers	square meters	1,000,000

Hot or Cold

Translating from degrees Celsius to degrees Fahrenheit (and back again) requires a little more than just multiplication.

- To go from °C to °F, multiply by 1.8, and then add 32
- To go from °F to °C, subtract 32 first, and then divide by 1.8

Extra credit

Now that you have had a chance to convert, measure up, and have some "Ah-ha!" and "D'oh!" moments, here's some extra credit to really stretch you. In math, "problems" are often considered mental playgrounds. Many practical applications and valuable insights have arisen from problems that were initially little more than cerebral games. Here are two teasers to try your math mettle and moxie! But please don't let the mystery make you feel muddled. It can take mathematicians centuries to solve problems like these and prove they have the right answer. (Remember Fermat's challenge?)

The Seven Bridges of Königsberg

Königsberg was once a Prussian city and is now called Kalingrad in Russia. The town contained two islands surrounded by the Pregel River and had seven connecting bridges. A question among the citizens of Königsberg was, *"Is it possible to tour the town by crossing each bridge once and only once and without missing a bridge?"* What do *you* say?

Happy touring!

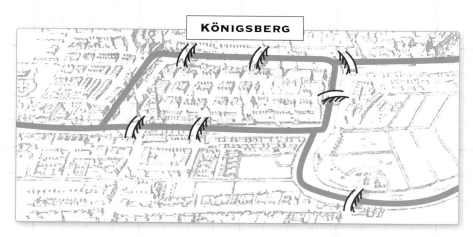

KÖNIGSBERG

Four-Color Map Theorem

This problem dates back to the mid-nineteenth century, when a cartographer in England noticed that he always seemed to be able to color in his maps with four colors or less. He wondered if more colors were ever needed. For the purposes of the exercise, he said, no territories that shared a common border could have the same color, although it was okay for territories that touched at only one point to be colored the same. With those terms, can you draw a map that requires five colors? Can you prove that four is the minimum number of colors ever needed?

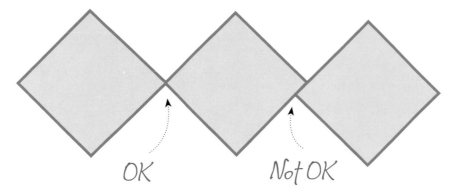

OK   Not OK

As for answers, if you try at all, you get the extra credit on these. Sometimes it's the journey, not the destination, right? These two problems are not the kind you can solve at home, but kudos to you for thinking about it! To find out what big time mathematicians did with these headscratchers, turn to page 138–139.

Arts 101

ARE THE MONA LISA, A KID'S FINGER PAINTING, BEETHOVEN'S 9TH, graffiti, and *La Traviata* all art? "Art" is a short word with long reaching power—a realm that represents creative forms of human communication, soul searching, enlightenment, and entertainment.

There are no equations for getting a right answer about the emotion of a sonata, no dictionary for how to interpret a sculpture, and no Periodic Table of Artists to chart a sculptor or painter's standing in the art world. Unlike more fact-oriented academic areas, the arts can be a rather subjective discipline. Many even debate what "art" is.

But studying and exploring the arts can help us see, hear, feel, and comprehend life more fully by both challenging and soothing our senses. The arts are the microscopes and telescopes of humanity's stories, and the mirrors and frames of our emotions and experiences, our nightmares and dreams.

For your own art appreciation, here are some eclectic peeks at pivotal painting, dance steps to keep you on your toes, rewarding movies that won awards, musicals to sing about, and architects to build on.

May the muses be with you!

Frames of Mind: Pivotal Painting

The phrase "art museum" usually conjures images of paintings on walls. Before the watercolors and oils were even framed, though, their creation often formed part of important cultural movements. In chronological order, here are a few Western examples of pivotal painting movements in the last two centuries that helped catalyze and capture change.

Hudson River School

Think dramatic lights and darks (a.k.a. *luminism*) in quintessentially American landscapes, such as the Adirondack and Catskill mountains and the Hudson River of New York. The Hudson River School refers to a fifty-year period (roughly 1825 to 1875) of artists who were important in forging an American style of painting, declaring artistic independence from Europe. The Hudson River School was not an educational institution, but a way of thinking about art. Painters, including Thomas Cole, Frederic Edwin Church, Albert Bierstadt, and George Inness, used the canvas to explore the spiritual ideas of Nature and God as one, and man's relationship to nature. While they probed with paintbrushes, the quills of American writers Ralph Waldo Emerson and James Fenimore Cooper delved into similar themes.

Indian Summer on the Hudson River (1861) by Albert Bierstadt (1830–1902).

Impressionism

Impressionism started with a group of mid-nineteenth-century painters in Paris whose works were rejected for breaking with the artistic traditions of the time. Painters who were turned down by France's famous juried exhibition, the *Salon de Paris*, were then invited by Napoleon III to showcase their works at a new *Salon des Refusés* (Salon of the Refused) in 1863.

A critic who saw the exhibition dismissed a painting by Claude Monet called *Impression: Sunrise* as unfinished, calling it no more than an "impression." The insult was turned into a goal for some painters—to give the impression of something, instead of trying to realistically portray it the way previous landscape and formal portrait painters would have done.

Impressionists also did not choose huge sweeping Biblical or historic moments for their canvases, but objects and moments from everyday life, things immortalized in now famous paintings of fruit, haystacks, and average people sitting at a café. Brushstrokes were still visible in the finished works, colors were applied wet and side by side instead of mixed together, and changes in light and motion were shown. Mary Cassatt, Paul Cézanne, Edgar Degas, Edouard Manet, Claude Monet, Camille Pissarro, Pierre-Auguste Renoir, and James Whistler are all considered "impressionists."

Grainstack at Sunset (1890–91) by Claude Monet (1840–1926) is an example of an impressionist painting.

{ **fyi** }

For not the first or last time, technology affected art during the impressionist period. The new availability of premixed paints in tubes liberated the impressionist painters from the labors of making their own paints, and enabled them to work more freely both indoors and outdoors (*en plein air*).

Cubism

Cubism was a short-lived movement (1908–1920) with an impact that revolutionized the art world. Artists of the era sought to move beyond depicting people, objects, and landscapes from a single perspective. Back in the Renaissance, painters made a huge leap when they moved beyond one flat dimension by using a single vanishing point to create a sense of depth and multiple dimensions. (Jump back to the math chapter on page 57, if you want to see how this works.) Cubists often tried to show things from several, often fractured, perspectives—sometimes as if several vanishing points were engaged. Cubist painters played with multiple angles,

Still Life with Fruit Dish and Mandolin (1919) by Juan Gris (1187–1927) is an example of cubism.

fragments, shapes, color juxtapositions, and layers to create a new look. The two most famous cubists were the Spaniard Pablo Picasso and the Frenchman Georges Braque. The styles of Paul Cézanne and Georges Seurat were some of their inspirations. In addition, Joan Miró, Piet Mondrian, Marcel Duchamp, and Marc Chagall were all cubist painters at some period in their careers.

Surrealism

Surrealist painters sought to go beyond the ordinary surface reality of an object and find a deeper psychological meaning. Think of René Magritte's portrait of a man with an apple in front of his face, or Salvador Dalí's wilting clocks on the landscape. Frida Kahlo, Max Ernst, Hieronymus Bosch, Joan Miró, and Man Ray had diverse styles but all have been called surrealists, as they experimented with unusual juxtapositions of images and color on canvas.

Art collector and patron Peggy Guggenheim married surrealist Max Ernst in 1930, and spurred surrealism painting on. For André Breton, the founder of the larger leftist philosophical movement of Surrealism in the 1920s, painting was secondary to politics and philosophy. Surrealism often aimed for the automatic expression of human thought without censors or reason.

Pop Art

Remember Andy Warhol's giant Campbell's tomato soup can? It's probably one of the most iconic symbols of pop art. Pop art used and manipulated images of popular culture and mass consumerism, often isolating an object from its context. Subjects included celebrities and images from billboards and even the comics, portrayed ironically and with a sense of parody. Hard lines and realism were often the style. Pop art aimed to be popular with the masses, not the art world's elite.

The Pasadena Art Museum in California gets credit for the first exhibit of pop art in America, a show called "New Painting of Common Objects" in 1962. Pop art's glory days in the United States were the experimental and tumultuous 1960s in New York. In addition to Warhol, Jasper Johns, Roy Lichtenstein, Robert Rauschenberg, and David Hockney are all touted as influential pop artists.

Build It, and They Will Come

Western architecture has come a long way since the Ionic, Doric, and Corinthian columns of the Greeks and the flying buttresses of Gothic times. For some, the evolutions unite the best of art and engineering, a happy marriage of creativity and emerging materials and technologies. For others, the newer blueprints and buildings are way past the "good olde days" when it comes to the artifices of edifices.

Here are a few of the Western shape-changers for the skylines of our cities and the rooflines of our homes.

Frank Gehry (1929–)

Frank Gehry (born Ephraim Owen Goldberg) is an international architect of contemporary curves in titillating titanium. People seem to either love or hate his distinctive work, starting with the Guggenheim Museum Bilbao

Walt Disney Concert Hall in Los Angeles, designed by Frank Gehry, opened in 2003.

in the Basque part of Spain through the Disney Hall in Los Angeles and the Experience Music Project in Seattle. The sweeping, sails-in-the-winds surfaces leave some folks soaring and others swearing. Unlike some outside-the-box architects, Gehry has a reputation for staying close to budget. He received the coveted Pritzker Architecture Prize in 1989, and he has reached the celebrity status of "starchitect," with many of his creations now popular tourist attractions in his own lifetime.

Frank Lloyd Wright (1867–1959)

If the word had existed then, Frank Lloyd Wright would have been a starchitect in his own time, alluring or alarming people with his originality and influence. The Guggenheim Museum in New York, the Fallingwater house near Pittsburgh, and the Hollyhock and Ennis houses in southern California are just a few of the more than four hundred buildings designed by Wright, most of which still stand. He created "Prairie" houses, with long flat lines, and "Usonian" houses for people of moderate income. Wright loved to integrate the nature of a location to forge "organic architecture" both inside and outside homes and buildings.

His mother was a dominant influence in his life and work. Even before he was born, she predicted he would make great buildings, and when he was a child, she gave him geometric blocks to play with. Wright's school in Arizona, Taliesin West, continues to give promising architects more than blocks for buildings.

Le Corbusier (1887–1965)

A leader in Modern architecture, or the International style, Le Corbusier was born in Switzerland, became a French citizen in 1930, and designed buildings that were constructed in Russia, India, central Europe, South America, and North America. Like Gehry, he, too, changed his name and was famous during his own lifetime. Born as Charles-Édouard Jeanneret-Gris, he renamed himself in 1920 as an example of how people could reinvent themselves. He also wanted to reinvent dense cities and urban architecture to create a better quality of life for the citizens.

Le Corbusier knocked down some mental and literal walls when he opened up floor plans. He also helped build the modern era with the use of reinforced concrete. As well as being an architect, he was also a painter, furniture-maker, and mythmaker, who died swimming in the Mediterranean.

Julia Morgan (1872–1957)

The infamous Hearst Castle, visited by over 35 million people in San Simeon, California, is the best known of Julia Morgan's seven hundred buildings. She earned a civil engineering degree from Berkeley in 1894, became the first woman to garner an architecture degree from the prestigious École des Beaux-Arts in Paris, and then was the first woman to be licensed as an architect in California. Early in her career, she created the El Campanil bell tower at Mills College in Oakland, constructed from the new material of reinforced concrete. When it survived the devastation of the 1906 San Francisco earthquake, her notoriety increased. The four bells named Faith, Hope, Joy, and Peace still ring out on the campus, and many of the buildings she designed over the next five decades have also endured, including the *Los Angeles Examiner* building and multiple California YWCAs.

More Wild West

At a time when female architects were rare, Morgan's contemporary, Mary Colter (1869–1958), helped forge the "National Park Rustic" look with lasting buildings of natural stone along the rim of the Grand Canyon. Like Frank Lloyd Wright, she tended to focus on interior details as well as the exterior of projects. The La Fonda hotel in New Mexico still shows some of her inside creativity. While Wright was incorporating Prairie themes in the Midwest, Colter integrated Native American motifs as well as Spanish and Mexican heritage into the Southwest buildings for the Fred Harvey chain of hotels and other clients.

Sir Christopher Wren (1632–1723)

Both Newton and Pascal thought he was a brilliant scientist, mathematician, and inventor. Christopher Wren also became one of the most influential and famous architects in English history. If it hadn't been for a bakery fire that ultimately destroyed most of London in 1666, Wren might not have had the opportunity to apply his architectural genius. After the fire, he designed or helped design more than fifty London churches. Before the fire, he was a professor of astronomy and a founder of the distinguished Royal Society, still in existence today.

Charles II appointed him as King's Surveyor of the Works in 1669. In those days, designing buildings was often regarded as applied mathematics because it utilized geometric shapes, ratios, and calculations. Wren contributed to the Royal Observatory at Greenwich, the Royal Hospital Chelsea (still in service), and the magnificent Saint Paul's Cathedral, where, several hundred years later, people still attend services. After his death at age ninety, Wren was buried in St. Paul's with a nearby inscription in Latin that translated to "Reader, if you seek his memorial, look around you."

Saint Paul's Cathedral in London was designed by Sir Christopher Wren
in the seventeenth century.

- Christopher Wren was featured on the fifty pound note issued by the Bank of London from 1991 to 2001. A crater on Mars is named after him.

- A picture of Le Corbusier adorned the Swiss 10-franc note issued in 1996.

- A US two-cent Frank Lloyd Wright stamp was issued in 1966 on his birthday, June 8.

Bits of Ballet

Art is often moving, especially if you try it yourself. There are five classic feet and arm positions in ballet, and fortunately for those who don't like memorizing names, they are called *first position, second position, third position, fourth position*, and *fifth position*. The fifth position of feet actually has three different arm positions, but they have easy to remember names, too: low, middle, and high fifth. Yes, the arms are low, at the middle, and high in the poses. The trick is being able to do it well.

First   Second   Third   Fourth   Fifth

The five feet positions in ballet.

It's said that the five feet positions in ballet may have started with Louis XIV, who pointed his feet outward to show off the bright buckles of his shoes when he performed a role in a court performance in 1681. The role also gave him an historic nickname: the Sun King.

For those who do like a moniker challenge, you can work on your French accent. *Glissade* is French for "sliding," and in ballet, it's a glide that starts and ends with the feet in the fifth position. *Plié* is "bent" in French, and in ballet, it refers to a movement with bent knees. *Arabesque* is a French word from the Italian going back to Latin meaning "from Arabs." In an arabesque, the ballet dancer stands on one straight leg and extends the other straight leg in the back with one extended arm.

Dance is better seen than read, but if you want to be *en pointe* for balletic conversation, the classics include the *Nutcracker, Swan Lake,* and *Giselle.*

And if someone is talking about the ballet of *Romeo and Juliet,* instead of jawing, "Oh yeah, that Shakespeare guy," you could ask, "The Prokofiev version or Tchaikovsky's?" Then go see them yourself and compare. Most ballets are set to great classical music, but much of classical music is without any dance performances.

Classical Notes

The history of Western classical music deserves at least a symphony, but here for our fast-paced world are a few measures *allegrissimo.* (*Allegrissimo* in music means "played really fast." It's also an Italian adjective for "cheerful.")

From Baroque to Romantic

The period from about 1600 to the beginning of the 1700s was often called the baroque period in classical music, and it saw the development of the opera, the concerto, and the concept of minor and major keys in modern music. Choral music dominated. Antonio Lucio Vivaldi and George Frideric Handel were seminal baroque composers.

From the early 1700s to the early 1800s, instrumental music was on the rise. While democracy was growing and the Enlightenment was unfolding in the Western world, the development of the symphony and quartet was giving structure to music without voices. The composers Johann Sebastian Bach, Franz Joseph Haydn, Wolfgang Amadeus Mozart, and Antonio Salieri all created lasting music in this period.

The nineteenth century brought Romanticism, a rebellion against the previous rules, and an embracing of emotions. The works of Robert Schumann,

Ludwig van Beethoven, Franz Schubert, Johannes Brahms, Franz Liszt, Frédéric Chopin, Hector Berlioz, and Felix Mendelssohn remain classics today.

The end of the nineteenth century began an era of great diversity for classical music: Claude Debussy, Igor Stravinsky, Sergei Prokofiev, Béla Bartók, and Sergei Rachmaninov all composed enduring masterpieces.

{ **fyi** }

- Bach, Handel, and Scarlatti were all born in 1685.

- Beethoven was a student of Haydn.

- Albert Schweitzer is more famous for his missionary work in Africa than for his music, but Schweitzer studied with Bach and spent six years writing about Bach and working on Bach's organ music.

Instrumentally Wonderful

Some classical music calls for choirs or quartets of instruments, but symphonies these days are best enjoyed with a full modern orchestra! Today's orchestra consists of five basic instrument sections: strings, brass, woodwinds, keyboards, and percussion.

Operas to Sing About

Some of the classical composers' most enduring work was opera.

- Wolfgang Amadeus **Mozart's** stage creations include *Marriage of Figaro, Don Giovanni,* and *The Magic Flute.*

- The operas of Giuseppe Fortunino Francesco **Verdi** include *Aida, La Traviata,* and *Rigoletto.*

- Giacomo **Puccini** composed *La Bohème, Tosca, Madame Butterfly,* and *Turandot.*

- The music for folk opera *Porgy and Bess* was created by George **Gershwin.**

Broadway's Longest-Running Hits

Phantom of the Opera has, to date, more than 9,500 performances since it began running in 1988. It has received seven Tony Awards and seven Drama Desk awards.

Cats had 7,485 performances from 1982 to 2000. It received seven Tonys and three Drama Desk Awards in 1983, and a Grammy for Best Cast Show Album in 1984.

Les Misérables had 6,680 performances from 1987 to 2003; the 2006 revival included 463 performances. It earned eight Tony Awards and five Drama Desk awards in 1987, and a Grammy in 1988.

A Chorus Line had 6,137 performances from 1975 to 1990; the 2006 revival added 759 performances. In 1976, it won nine Tony Awards, five Drama Desk Awards, and the Pulitzer Prize for Drama.

Oh! Calcutta! had 1,314 performances in 1969; the revival from 1976 to 1989 tallied 5,959 performances. It's Broadway's longest-running revue.

Other Broadway musicals that have topped five thousand performances include *Beauty and the Beast, Chicago, Rent,* and *The Lion King.*

Even though it was off-Broadway, a special standing ovation goes to the world's longest-running musical, *The Fantasticks,* for 17,162 performances from 1960 to 2002 in the Sullivan Street Playhouse in Greenwich Village.

The Broadway marquee for Les Misérables in New York City. Les Misérables claims it became the longest running musical in the world in 2006 when it celebrated its twenty-first birthday in London, ignoring The Fantasticks record.

Spotlight on American Theater

- The longest-running dramatic play on Broadway was *Life with Father*, with 3,224 performances between 1939 and 1947.
- Eugene O'Neill received the most Pulitzer Prizes for Drama—four. Edward Albee would have tied him, but the selection committee's choice for 1963, his *Who's Afraid of Virginia Woolf*, was negated by the advisory board on grounds of the play's use of naughty words and portrayal of sexual issues.
- Double dippers for Drama Pulitzers include Thornton Wilder, Tennessee Williams, August Wilson, Robert E. Sherwood, and George S. Kaufman.
- The most Tonys awarded to any non-musical Broadway show is seven, which went to *The Coast of Utopia* in 2007.

{ fyi }

The full name of Broadway's prestigious Tony Award is the Antoinette Perry Award for Excellence in Theater. Perry was a beloved actress, and directed and produced a play that won a Pulitzer—*Harvey*—shortly before her death.

Take Me to the Movies

Cave people may have played with shadow puppets on the wall while sitting around a campfire, but moving pictures as we know them today are a relatively new art form for an audience. Singing, dancing, and painting go back many millennia, but movies are the storytelling entertainment of modern times, both reflecting and shaping popular culture.

"And the Winners Are..."

Since 1927, the Academy of Motion Picture Arts and Sciences, based in California, has awarded an annual Academy Award for Best Picture. Some say "the Oscar" is awarded more for entertainment than for art, and more for politics than for profundity. Still, some great movies did get the golden nod of Oscar.

The Oscars for Best Picture

Year	Film	Year	Film
2010	The King's Speech	1981	Chariots of Fire
2009	The Hurt Locker	1980	Ordinary People
2008	Slumdog Millionaire	1979	Kramer vs. Kramer
2007	No Country for Old Men	1978	The Deer Hunter
2006	The Departed	1977	Annie Hall
2005	Crash	1976	Rocky
2004	Million Dollar Baby	1975	One Flew Over the Cuckoo's Nest
2003	The Lord of the Rings: The Return of the King	1974	The Godfather: Part II
		1973	The Sting
2002	Chicago	1972	The Godfather
2001	A Beautiful Mind	1971	The French Connection
2000	Gladiator	1970	Patton
1999	American Beauty	1969	Midnight Cowboy
1998	Shakespeare in Love	1968	Oliver!
1997	Titanic	1967	In the Heat of the Night
1996	The English Patient	1966	A Man for All Seasons
1995	Braveheart	1965	The Sound of Music
1994	Forrest Gump	1964	My Fair Lady
1993	Schindler's List	1963	Tom Jones
1992	Unforgiven	1962	Lawrence of Arabia
1991	The Silence of the Lambs	1961	West Side Story
1990	Dances with Wolves	1960	The Apartment
1989	Driving Miss Daisy	1959	Ben-Hur
1988	Rain Man	1958	Gigi
1987	The Last Emperor	1957	The Bridge on the River Kwai
1986	Platoon	1956	Around the World in 80 Days
1985	Out of Africa	1955	Marty
1984	Amadeus	1954	On the Waterfront
1983	Terms of Endearment	1953	From Here to Eternity
1982	Gandhi	1952	The Greatest Show on Earth

The Oscars for Best Picture (continued)

1951	*An American in Paris*	1939	*Gone with the Wind*
1950	*All About Eve*	1938	*You Can't Take It with You*
1949	*All the King's Men*	1937	*The Life of Emile Zola*
1948	*Hamlet*	1936	*The Great Ziegfeld*
1947	*Gentleman's Agreement*	1935	*Mutiny on the Bounty*
1946	*The Best Years of Our Lives*	1934	*It Happened One Night*
1945	*The Lost Weekend*	1933	*Cavalcade*
1944	*Going My Way*	1932	*Grand Hotel*
1943	*Casablanca*	1931	*Cimarron*
1942	*Mrs. Miniver*	1930	*All Quiet on the Western Front*
1941	*How Green Was My Valley*	1929	*The Broadway Melody*
1940	*Rebecca*	1927/1928	*Wings*

Screen Talk

Al Jolson said, "You ain't heard nothin' yet," in *The Jazz Singer* (1927), the first feature-length motion picture with dialogue. Since then, we've heard many more great lines that have become part of the way we communicate off the screen.

Guess which movies these lines are from. For extra points, generate your own discussions of whether the actors or writers should get credit for making the quotes famous.

1) "I coulda been a contender."

2) "Elementary, my dear Watson."

3) "There's no place like home."

4) "Go ahead, make my day."

5) "Follow the money."

6) "Show me the money."

7) "I'll be back."

8) "If you build it, he will come."

9) "May the Force be with you."

10) "Here's looking at you, kid."

11) "It's showtime!"

12) "I'm going to make him an offer he can't refuse."

13) "Frankly, my dear, I don't give a damn."

14) "They're here!"

15) "I'm the King of the World!"

16) "You talking to me?"

17) "My Precious."

18) "Life is a banquet, and most poor suckers are starving to death."

19) "I am mad as hell, and I am not going to take this anymore."

20) "Carpe Diem. Seize the day, boys. Make our lives extraordinary."

You can find the answers on page 139.

Extra credit

Sculptural Stumper

Now that you have hummed or *plié*d through some painting, dance, music, theater, and film, are you ready for sculpture, one of the oldest art forms?

Take a look at the famous sculptures on the next page and choose which of the following sculptors created them. Just to challenge you, there are more sculptor names than sculpture images to choose from!

- Michelangelo Buonarroti (Italian, 1475–1564)
- Frédéric-Auguste Bartholdi (French, 1834–1904)
- Donatello (Italian, 1386–1466)
- Praxiteles (Greek, 4th century BCE)
- Franz Xaver Messerschmidt (German-Austrian, 1736–1783)
- Auguste Rodin (French, 1840–1917)
- Eduardo Chillida (Spanish Basque, 1924–2002)
- Emmanuel Frémiet (French, 1824–1910)
- John Henry Foley (Irish, 1818–1874)

The matches of sculptors with their marble and metal are on page 140.

Now for extra, extra credit: go enjoy the art form you love most or go create something wonderful yourself!

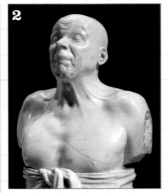

Social Studies 101

THE WORDS "SOCIAL STUDIES" MAY CONJURE UP CHILDHOOD MEMORIES of filling in maps with different-colored crayons, but the subject is much bigger than that. In a broad sense, Social Studies is about filling in our understanding of how societies function—the politics, economics, and social enterprises of cultures, individuals, and countries.

The social sciences comprise the giant arc of human interfaces with the world, and they include anthropology, economics, political science, education, communications, geography, and the law. (Two other very popular branches, psychology and history, get their own chapters elsewhere in this book.)

This chapter includes ways of looking at people in the United States from a global perspective, a statistical insight about deviancy, a little economic currency to keep you afloat, some types of leadership, and, for the nostalgic, even a map of state capitals!

Hello on the Go

Wherever you go, it pays to know how to say "hello."

- Arabic: *Marhaba*
- Australian: *G'day*
- Chamorro (Guam): *Hafa adai*
- Esperanto: *Saluton* (formal), *sal* (informal)
- French: *Salut* or *Bonjour*
- Hawaiian: *Aloha*
- Hebrew: *Shalom*
- Hindi: *Namaste*
- Italian: *Ciao*
- Japanese: *Oyaho gozaimasu* (in the morning)
- Mandarin Chinese: *Ni Hao*
- Russian: *Privet*
- Spanish: *Hola*
- Swahili: *Jambo*

Who Are We?

How do you think the US compares to the rest of the world when it comes to birth rates, life expectancy, and languages spoken? Numbers are one way to look at life and death issues and the social make-up of cultures.

	US	**World**
POPULATION		
	310,232,863 (2010 est.)	6,830,586,985 (2010 est.)
AGE STRUCTURE		
0–14 yrs	20.2%	27.2%
15–64 yrs	67%	65.2%
65 yrs and over	12.8% (2009 est.)	7.6%
MEDIAN AGE		
Total	36.7 yrs.	28.4 yrs.
Male	35.4 yrs.	27.7 yrs.
Female	38 yrs. (2009 est.)	29 yrs. (2009 est.)
POPULATION GROWTH RATE	0.977% (2009 est.)	1.133% (2009 est.)
BIRTH RATE (births/1,000 population)	13.83 (2010 est.)	19.86 (2009 est.)
DEATH RATE (deaths/1,000 population)	8.38 (2010 est.)	8.37 (2009 est.)
URBANIZATION		
Urban population	82% (2008)	50.5% (2010)
Rate of urbanization	1.3% annual rate of change (2005–2010 est.)	
	1.85% annual rate of change (2010–2015 est.)	
SEX RATIO (male/female)		
Total	0.97 (2009 est.)	1.01 (2009 est.)
At birth	1.05	1.07
Under 15 yrs	1.04	1.06
15–64 yrs	1	1.02
65 yrs and over	0.75	0.78

Who Are We? (continued)

	US	World
INFANT MORTALITY RATE		
(deaths/1,000 live births)		
Total	6.14 (2010 est.)	44.13 (2009 est.)
Male	6.81	46.19
Female	5.44	41.92
LIFE EXPECTANCY AT BIRTH		
Total	78.11 yrs. (2009 est.)	66.12 yrs. (2009 est.)
Male	75.65 yrs.	64.29 yrs.
Female	80.69 yrs.	68.07 yrs.
FERTILITY RATE		
(children born/woman)	2.05 (2009 est.)	2.56 (2009 est.)
HIV/AIDS		
Adult prevalence rate	0.6% (2007 est.)	0.8% (2007 est.)
People living with HIV/AIDS	1.2 million (2007 est.)	33 million (2007 est.)
Deaths	22,000 (2007 est.)	2 million (2007 est.)

LANGUAGES *(Note: percents are for "first language" speakers only)*

	US	World	
English	82.1%	Mandarin Chinese	13.22%
Spanish	10.7%	Spanish	4.88%
Other Indo-European	3.8%	English	4.68%
Asian and Pacific island	2.7%	Arabic	3.12%
(Note: Hawaiian is an official language in Hawaii)		Hindi	2.74%
Other	0.7% (2000 census)	Portuguese	2.69%
		Bengali	2.59%
		Russian	2.2%
		Japanese	1.85%
		Standard German	1.44%
		French	1.2% (2005 est.)

	US	World
LITERACY		
(def: age 15 and over and can read and write)		
Total	99%	82%
Male	99%	87%
Female	99% (2003 est.)	77% (2005 est)

Source: CIA World Factbook

Head(s) of State

Should government have limited or full control? Is leadership divinely bestowed, hereditary, elected by the people, or claimed by the military? There are 192 different nation members in the United Nations, as of 2010, and each has its own form of government.

To help you use your head about various Heads of State, here's a glossary explaining some of the kinds of government and political systems in the world. You may astutely note that there is some overlap. Some countries have more than one form of government. The United States is a federal republic. Would you say its form of government is also presidential? And constitutional? And democratic?

The following definitions to enhance your own intelligence are courtesy of the Central Intelligence Agency of the United States, culled verbatim from the *CIA World Factbook (2009)*.

ABSOLUTE MONARCHY: a form of government where the monarch rules unhindered, i.e., without any laws, constitution, or legally organized opposition.

ANARCHY: a condition of lawlessness or political disorder brought about by the absence of governmental authority.

AUTHORITARIAN: a form of government in which state authority is imposed onto many aspects of citizens' lives.

COMMONWEALTH: a nation, state, or other political entity founded on law and united by a compact of the people for the common good.

"A government big enough to give you everything you want is big enough to take everything you have." —Gerald Ford

{ **fyi** }

Between 1990 and 2009, thirty-three new countries were added to the world count. The breakup of the USSR and Yugoslavia created new sovereign nations.

COMMUNIST: a system of government in which the state plans and controls the economy and a single—often authoritarian—party holds power; state controls are imposed with the elimination of private ownership of property or capital, while claiming to make progress toward a higher social order in which all goods are equally shared by the people (i.e., a classless society).

"It is true that liberty is precious; so precious that it must be carefully rationed." —Lenin

CONFEDERACY (CONFEDERATION): a union by compact or treaty between states, provinces, or territories that creates a central government with limited powers; the constituent entities retain supreme authority over all matters except those delegated to the central government.

CONSTITUTIONAL: a government by or operating under an authoritative document (constitution) that sets forth the system of fundamental laws and principles that determines the nature, functions, and limits of that government.

CONSTITUTIONAL DEMOCRACY: a form of government in which the sovereign power of the people is spelled out in a governing constitution.

CONSTITUTIONAL MONARCHY: a system of government in which a monarch is guided by a constitution whereby his/her rights, duties, and responsibilities are spelled out in written law or by custom.

DEMOCRACY: a form of government in which the supreme power is retained by the people, but which is usually exercised indirectly through a system of representation and delegated authority periodically renewed.

DEMOCRATIC REPUBLIC: a state in which the supreme power rests in the body of citizens entitled to vote for officers and representatives responsible to them.

DICTATORSHIP: a form of government in which a ruler or small clique wield absolute power (not restricted by a constitution or laws).

ECCLESIASTICAL: a government administered by a church.

EMIRATE: similar to a monarchy or sultanate, but a government in which the supreme power is in the hands of an emir (the ruler of a Muslim state); the emir may be an absolute overlord or a sovereign with constitutionally limited authority.

FEDERAL (FEDERATION): a form of government in which sovereign power is formally divided—usually by means of a constitution—between a central authority and a number of constituent regions (states, colonies, or provinces) so that each region retains some management of its internal affairs; differs from a confederacy in that the central government exerts influence directly upon both individuals as well as upon the regional units.

FEDERAL REPUBLIC: a state in which the powers of the central government are restricted and in which the component parts (states, colonies, or provinces) retain a degree of self-government; ultimate sovereign power rests with the voters who chose their governmental representatives.

ISLAMIC REPUBLIC: a particular form of government adopted by some Muslim states; although such a state is, in theory, a theocracy, it remains a republic, but its laws are required to be compatible with the laws of Islam.

Naming an Unqualified Government

The following form of government is not listed in the CIA handbook, but is in dictionaries.

Kakistocracy is a real word, meaning a government ruled by the worst people, those least capable and qualified.

MAOISM: the theory and practice of Marxism-Leninism developed in China by Mao Zedong (Mao Tse-tung), which states that a continuous revolution is necessary if the leaders of a communist state are to keep in touch with the people.

MARXISM: the political, economic, and social principles espoused by nineteenth-century economist Karl Marx; he viewed the struggle of workers as a progression of historical forces that would proceed from a class struggle of the proletariat (workers) exploited by capitalists (business owners), to a socialist "dictatorship of the proletariat," to, finally, a classless society—communism.

MARXISM-LENINISM: an expanded form of communism developed by Lenin from doctrines of Karl Marx; Lenin saw imperialism as the final stage of capitalism and shifted the focus of workers' struggle from developed to underdeveloped countries.

MONARCHY: the supreme power is lodged in the hands of a monarch who reigns over a state or territory, usually for life and by hereditary right; the monarch may be either a sole absolute ruler or a sovereign—such as a king, queen, or prince—with constitutionally limited authority.

OLIGARCHY: a government in which control is exercised by a small group of individuals whose authority generally is based on wealth or power.

PARLIAMENTARY DEMOCRACY: a political system in which the legislature (parliament) selects the government—a prime minister, premier, or chancellor along with the cabinet ministers—according to party strength as expressed in elections; by this system, the government acquires a dual responsibility—to the people as well as to the parliament.

PARLIAMENTARY GOVERNMENT (Cabinet-Parliamentary government): a government in which members of an executive branch (the cabinet and its leader: a prime minister, premier, or chancellor) are nominated to their positions by a legislature or parliament, and are directly responsible to it; this type of government can be dissolved at will by the parliament (legislature) by means of a no confidence vote, or the leader of the cabinet may dissolve the parliament if it can no longer function.

PARLIAMENTARY MONARCHY: a state headed by a monarch who is not actively involved in policy formation or implementation (i.e., the exercise of sovereign powers by a monarch in a ceremonial capacity); true governmental leadership is carried out by a cabinet and its head—a prime minister, premier, or chancellor—who are drawn from a legislature (parliament).

PRESIDENTIAL: a system of government where the executive branch exists separately from a legislature (to which it is generally not accountable).

REPUBLIC: a representative democracy in which the people's elected deputies (representatives), not the people themselves, vote on legislation.

SOCIALISM: a government in which the means of planning, producing, and distributing goods is controlled by a central government that theoretically seeks a more just and equitable distribution of property and labor; in actuality, most socialist governments have ended up being no more than dictatorships over workers by a ruling elite.

SULTANATE: similar to a monarchy, but in which the supreme power is in the hands of a sultan (the head of a Muslim state); the sultan may be an absolute ruler or a sovereign with constitutionally limited authority.

THEOCRACY: a government in which a Deity is recognized as the supreme civil ruler, but the Deity's laws are interpreted by ecclesiastical authorities (bishops, mullahs, etc.); a government subject to religious authority.

TOTALITARIAN: a government that seeks to subordinate the individual to the state by controlling not only all political and economic matters, but also the attitudes, values, and beliefs of its population.

A Capital Idea

Do you remember learning all the state capitals of the US in elementary school? How many can you name now? Can you do it in alphabetical order?

A state capital isn't always the biggest city in the state; only seventeen are also their states' most populated cities. Nor is the capital always the most centrally located. Some capitals even border other states. But a state's capital is the state's center of government, and that's usually where the power resides. So here's a novel Power Point presentation, no computer required.

In the map on page 88, each state has a point where its capital is located, along with a number. Write the number of the corresponding state next to the name of its capital on the list. How many "Power Points" can you match with the right capitals?

{ **fyi** }

The largest state capital in geographic size is Juneau, Alaska. The largest state capital by municipal population is Phoenix, Arizona. Vermont's capital, Montpelier, has fewer people than any other state capital.

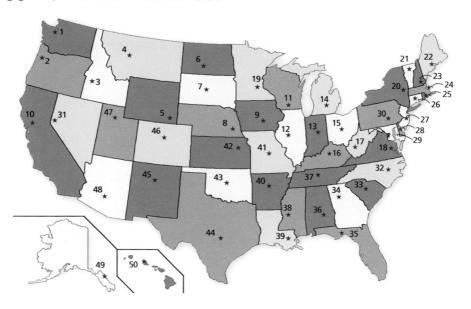

Power Points

Write in the number of the corresponding state capital.

US Capitals	US Capitals	US Capitals
Albany_____	Dover_____	Oklahoma City_____
Annapolis_____	Frankfort_____	Olympia_____
Atlanta_____	Harrisburg_____	Phoenix_____
Augusta_____	Hartford_____	Pierre_____
Austin_____	Helena_____	Providence_____
Baton Rouge_____	Honolulu_____	Raleigh_____
Bismarck_____	Indianapolis_____	Richmond_____
Boise_____	Jackson_____	Sacramento_____
Boston_____	Jefferson City_____	Saint Paul_____
Carson City_____	Juneau _____	Salem_____
Charleston_____	Lansing _____	Salt Lake City_____
Cheyenne_____	Lincoln _____	Santa Fe_____
Columbia_____	Little Rock _____	Springfield_____
Columbus_____	Madison _____	Tallahassee_____
Concord_____	Montgomery_____	Topeka_____
Denver_____	Montpelier_____	Trenton_____
Des Moines_____	Nashville _____	

Answers

State	Capital	#	State	Capital	#
Alabama	Montgomery	36	Montana	Helena	4
Alaska	Juneau	49	Nebraska	Lincoln	8
Arizona	Phoenix	48	Nevada	Carson City	31
Arkansas	Little Rock	40	New Hampshire	Concord	23
California	Sacramento	10	New Jersey	Trenton	27
Colorado	Denver	46	New Mexico	Santa Fe	45
Connecticut	Hartford	26	New York	Albany	20
Delaware	Dover	28	North Carolina	Raleigh	32
Florida	Tallahassee	35	North Dakota	Bismarck	6
Georgia	Atlanta	34	Ohio	Columbus	15
Hawaii	Honolulu	50	Oklahoma	Oklahoma City	43
Idaho	Boise	3	Oregon	Salem	2
Illinois	Springfield	12	Pennsylvania	Harrisburg	30
Indiana	Indianapolis	13	Rhode Island	Providence	25
Iowa	Des Moines	9	South Carolina	Columbia	33
Kansas	Topeka	42	South Dakota	Pierre	7
Kentucky	Frankfort	16	Tennessee	Nashville	37
Louisiana	Baton Rouge	39	Texas	Austin	44
Maine	Augusta	22	Utah	Salt Lake City	47
Maryland	Annapolis	29	Vermont	Montpelier	21
Massachusetts	Boston	24	Virginia	Richmond	18
Michigan	Lansing	14	Washington	Olympia	1
Minnesota	Saint Paul	19	West Virginia	Charleston	17
Mississippi	Jackson	38	Wisconsin	Madison	11
Missouri	Jefferson City	41	Wyoming	Cheyenne	5

Economists Who Made Change

Adam Smith (1723–1790)

Best known for his five-book series, *The Wealth of Nations*, this Scottish economist is often given the title "father of modern economics." Smith is credited with coining the phrase "the invisible hand," the idea that self-regulation can work given his theories supporting free trade, free market, and the belief that self-interest best serves the greater good. In 1776, he wrote that the cost of maintaining colonies in America as a market for British goods was not worth the expense and effort.

Thomas Robert Malthus (1766–1834)

Before the Industrial Revolution, Reverend Malthus studied the interactions between food supply and population growth. He was intrigued by how people survived, despite numeric projections. Basically, he determined that food supply growth was slower than population growth, so people would starve to death if it weren't for other moral or natural factors (like later marriages, a poorer health-care system, natural disasters, and war). His longer-term evolutionary look at economics influenced Darwin and is still discussed today.

John Stuart Mill (1806–1873)

Mill may be best known for his book on ethics, *Utilitarianism*, which espoused the "greatest good for the greatest number of people," or what is sometimes called the "greatest happiness theory." His *Principles of Political Economy*, however, was one of the most read books on economics, both in Mill's own time and for decades beyond his death, influencing the teaching of economics at universities, including at Oxford. He opposed slavery and defended the rights of women to be educated and to work.

Karl Heinrich Marx (1818–1883)

The German author of both *Das Kapital* (a look at the political economy of capitalism) and *The Communist Manifesto* (with Friedrich Engels), Marx saw history as a series of class struggles. He believed that in capitalism the laborer or worker who produced goods was underappreciated and in conflict with the people who owned the capital. In the evolution of systems, just as capitalism had replaced feudalism, he suggested that capitalism would be replaced by socialism, and then communism.

John Maynard Keynes (1883–1946)

Keynes was a celebrity in his own time, a member of the literary Bloomsbury Group (See Literature & Grammar, page 29), and a groundbreaking economist. In his *General Theory of Employment, Interest and Money*, Keynes countered the prevalent balanced-budget approach and posited that the government should deficit-spend to help achieve full employment during difficult times. In the US, this thinking contributed to the government's decision to hire people for public works endeavors during the Depression.

Money Talk

What's the difference between the cost of living and opportunity cost? The GNP and GDP? Macroeconomics and microeconomics? A leopard and a dugong?* Supply and demand? If you already know this stuff, you should cut this mini-class now!

GNP and GDP

The Gross National Product (GNP) measures the value of what is produced in a country. It's the sum dollar figure of all the goods and services made for consumption during a set time—goods being material things such as cars, soccer balls, food, and flower pots, and services being work that people perform, such as medical care, transportation, education, law enforcement, and communications.

*Okay, just checking to see if you were really reading all this. A leopard is a member of the cat family, and the dugong is a marine mammal. Neither studies economics. Getting this one right earns you lots of extra credit, but not in economics.

Gross Domestic Product (GDP) gauges the value of what is produced within a country, so income earned overseas and imports don't count. GDP includes the output of both labor and property and is an international device for comparing economies. There are product, income, and expenditure methods to calculate GDP.

Micro- and Macroeconomics

"Micro" is a prefix originating from the Greek, meaning "very small," so it's no surprise that microeconomics looks at the *parts* of the economy, such as how prices, production, and distribution affect one another. Microeconomics also examines individual markets and industries.

"Macro"—also from Greek—translates as a prefix meaning "long" or "large," so macroeconomics looks at the *whole* economics of a system or country, such as the rate of employment or the GDP (see above).

Costs—of Living and Opportunity

The cost of living is your basic food, shelter, and clothing expenses needed to maintain a certain standard of living. It's usually calculated by the average costs of a preselected list of goods and services during a given period.

Opportunity cost doesn't show up on budgets or corporate statements, but it can influence decision-making. Your opportunity cost factors in the losses of any option B opportunities that result from selecting option A over B when A and B are mutually exclusive. What money/time/pleasure are you missing by not choosing the other option? If you spend your one hundred dollars of birthday money on a dog instead of a tree, your opportunity cost is the tree and its benefits.

Equilibrium

In economics, equilibrium occurs when supply equals demand. Sellers produce and provide an equal amount of goods and services (supply) to what buyers want and purchase (demand).

When a price drops below this equilibrium, there is a shortage in supply. (If the price of something suddenly goes down, more people will presumably buy it and the supply will no longer be adequate.) Conversely, if the price rises above the equilibrium point, fewer people will buy, and a surplus results.

Anthropology: The Human Story

When you hear the word *anthropology,* do you think of Margaret Mead researching in Samoa, Louis and Mary Leakey searching for the earliest human remains in Africa, Thor Heyerdahl crossing the ocean on the Kon-Tiki raft, or Indiana Jones tearing up the movie screen?

The term *anthropology,* Greek for "study of humans," was first used in 1593, but the story really starts long, long, long ago when humans were emerging onto the landscape. The four basic fields of anthropology span the humanities and the sciences. Anthropologists look for the weird and the normal, and the aberrant and the universal. Different kinds of anthropology can provide us with engaging mirrors for the human species through time and place.

Archaeology

From uncovering pre-historic human bones in Kenya to going through modern garbage in Oklahoma, archaeologists examine the material goods and artifacts of a culture for clues and data. Since most of the human time on Earth is prehistoric (meaning before writing), archaeology is a powerful way to "dig in" for insights.

What do these rocks have to do with anthropology? Lithic core is an artifact that comes from the act of lithic reduction, which may have been used to rough out a knife or tool. These are on display at the Museum of Toulouse in France.

Cultural Anthropology

Sometimes called *ethnology,* cultural anthropology looks at the institutions of a culture—the family structures, kinship, descent, economics, religions, and forms of leadership and communication. Cultural anthropologists compile their findings in ethnographies, which are written studies of a culture.

Biological Anthropology

From studying fellow primates (think Jane Goodall with the chimps) to the human genome project, biological anthropology looks at biology (i.e., sex, health, genes, and evolution) to learn about what makes us humans human, and how we differ from other cultures, ages, times, and species.

Linguistic Anthropology

What is the relationship between language and culture? How do people use language (verbal and nonverbal)? How does language change over time and what does that say about the speakers? If you want answers to these kinds of questions, linguistic anthropology is the quest for you.

Sociology: Are You a Deviant?

In most arenas of life, you don't want to be a deviant. When sociologists look at the bell curves of distribution, most people are in the middle, and "deviants" are the two extremes, at both ends of the continuum—the really poor and the really rich, the really unhappy and the really happy, the really weak minded and the really smart. So maybe it's time to change your goal, in some cases: become a good deviant! Do you think the phrase "That's really deviant!" will ever catch on as high praise?

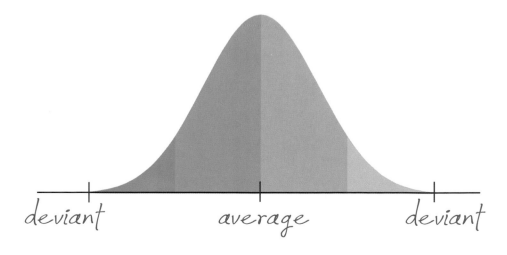

deviant   average   deviant

Extra Credit

Big and Small

To some people, size matters.

1. What are the five largest nations in the world?

2. What are the five smallest nations?

3. How many square miles is the natural world?

4. How much surface area of our planet is water and how much is land?

Assign points for each correct answer in advance, and then decide what the "opportunity cost" would be if you answer these questions instead of going on to the next chapter. If you get all the answers correct, you deserve to rule your own country and choose its form of government. Your motto could be "That's really deviant!"

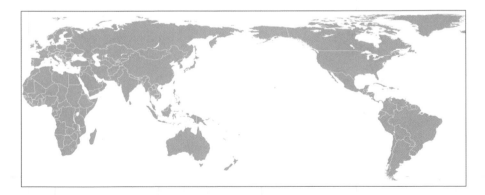

The answers, large and small, are on page 140.

Science 101

 IF YOU'VE EVER OBSERVED A PHENOMENON IN NATURE AND ASKED "Why?" or watched a hummingbird, racecar, or crashing wave and wondered how it works, then you have taken the first steps on the path of science. Science begins with questions and continues with quests for answers, and then follows with testing and proving ideas with thought and evidence. And then there are more questions.

From the time of the ancient Greeks, curious people who sought explainable answers were "natural philosophers." The actual word "scientist" was not coined until the 1830s. Until then, it was often the mathematicians who used their language of numbers and logic to explain how phenomena like gravity and energy work.

When Sir Isaac Newton wrote one of the most important and revolutionary science books ever, *Philosophiæ Naturalis Principia Mathematica*, first available in 1687, he deliberately wrote the work in Latin. He also told a friend that he made it difficult to understand "to avoid being baited by little Smatterers in Mathematicks."

These days, it's hard to feel close to being even a Smatterer in *any* area of science. It's difficult to keep up with just the *names* of emerging fields in science, let alone the content. For example, pharmocogenetics is the study of how genetics affects the body's response to drugs, and neuroecology explores how the nervous system of an organism interacts with its specific environment. It seems like humans learn more about how big and how small everything is every year.

Here, then, are just some smatterings (in English, not Latin!). You can start in galaxies far, far away and end with some spin on the oceans on your home planet, after checking out some quirky guys and some cool discoveries and theories.

High Lights Above

Galaxies Galore

In 1919, at the end of WWI, scientists only knew of *one* galaxy—our Milky Way. Now they estimate there are more than 100 billion galaxies in the observable universe, or maybe even hundreds of billions of galaxies! That's at least 100,000,000,000 galaxies! Multiply that by, say, 200,000,000,000 stars each, and you have a lot of stars (and a lot of zeros.) For an even larger astronomical number, imagine if most of those stars, like our sun, have planets!

Halley's Comet

Appearing every seventy-five to seventy-six years, Halley's is the only "periodic" comet visible to the naked eye. The elliptically orbiting comet was named after Edmund Halley (1656–1742), the great scientist who catalyzed Newton to write the *Principia*. Halley then actually funded and edited the

Comet (Donati) on October 5, 1858. Note the Big Dipper to the right.

pivotal work. He sparked others too: His knowledge of the transit of Venus prompted Captain Cook's expedition to Tahiti. Halley was also an adventurer himself, once heading to the Southern Hemisphere where he charted more than 340 previously unmapped stars.

By the way, it's thought that the great mind pronounced his last name like HALL-ee, rhyming with *Bali*. It did not rhyme with *Bailey*, as many Americans pronounce it, nor with *valley*, as the Brits often say his name.

"Every great advance in science has issued from a new audacity of imagination." —John Dewey

Titanic Above Water

The universe is full of gases and solids, but only Earth was known to have liquids until scientists found something mysterious in a lake on Saturn's largest moon, Titan. Don't buy a Saturnian bathing suit yet, though. The liquid found by the spacecraft Cassini in 2008 was *hydrocarbon* based, not water, and it's very cold in that part of the galaxy. Since then, there have been exciting discoveries of more drinkable water on our own moon, for some closer liquid lunacy!

Shooting Stars

A shooting star is not a star, but it might be a piece of the moon or Mars— or cosmic trash. Here's how to tell your *meteoroids* from your *meteors* and *meteorites*. Ready?

A *meteoroid* is rocky or metallic space debris, sometimes only as big as a pebble. It becomes a *meteor* when falling through the atmosphere of the earth. A meteor is often called a "shooting star" or "falling star" because of the quick streak of bright light generated from friction when it hits the earth's denser atmosphere.

If it doesn't burn up entirely and it lands on Earth, it's called a *meteorite*. There are only about a hundred known meteorites a year, but some nights you can see hundreds of meteors shoot across the sky. It's unscientific, but many cultures believe that if you wish upon a meteor (a shooting star), your wish will come true.

Big Dipper

Seven stars that light the night sky year-round in the Northern Hemisphere are known as the Big Dipper in the United States and the Plough in Great Britain. Many know that two of its stars point to Polaris, or the "North Star," which helps navigators as a visual cue to true north. All other stars appear to rotate during the night and through the seasons around the relatively fixed Polaris.

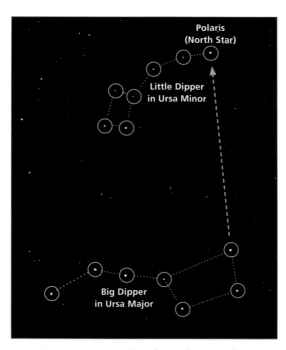

Do you want to head north at night? Here's one way to find the North Star when you are in most of North America.

The Big Dipper is part of the constellation Ursa Major, also known as the the Great Bear, which has been in the mythology of many cultures since ancient times. Stars in Ursa Major point to the North Star, which is in the constellation Ursa Minor (the Little Dipper, or Little Bear).

Fantastic Discoveries

Nanotechnology: It's a Small World

Think very, very, very small. Nanotechnology deals with the study, manipulation, and applications of single atoms and molecules. A nanometer is one-billionth of a meter—that's 1/1,000,000,000 of a meter. A common comparison of a

Size Matters

Prefix	Symbol	Quantity
yotta	Y	10^{24}
zetta	Z	10^{21}
exa	E	10^{18}
peta	P	10^{15}
tera	T	10^{12}
giga	G	10^{9}
mega	M	10^{6}
kilo	k	10^{3}
hecto	h	10^{2}
deca	da	10^{1}
one basic unit	10^{0}	
deci	d	10^{-1}
centi	c	10^{-2}
milli	m	10^{-3}
micro	µ	10^{-6}
nano	n	10^{-9}
pico	p	10^{-12}
femto	f	10^{-15}
atto	a	10^{-18}
zepto	z	10^{-21}
yocto	y	10^{-24}

What, no grouchos, chicos, and harpos?

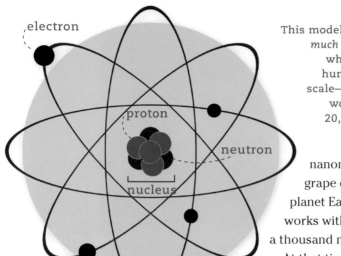

electron

proton

neutron

nucleus

This model of an atom is of course *much* larger than a real atom, which can't be seen by the human eye. It also is not to scale—if it were, the electrons would be off the page and 20,000 times further away!

nanometer to a meter is a grape or marble to the entire planet Earth. Nanotechnology works with matter smaller than a thousand nanometers.

At that tiny scale, the properties of elements can change, including the way gravity affects them. What could happen when atoms learn to "self-assemble"? What synthetic atoms could be made? How will manufacturing and medicine and myriad other parts of our lives change if humans master the very small? The potential delights and dangers are just beginning to emerge. Are you ready for yoctotechnology?

Extremophiles to the Max

If you remember being taught that photosynthesis from the sun was required for life on this planet, you are dating yourself. It turns out some creatures are able to live far from the light of day and night—down in thermal vents in the oceans and in black-out sulfur caves, and there are bacteria that thrive in temperatures hotter and colder than previously imagined suitable for existence. Life prevails in the deep ocean under intense pressures, and it persists in a vacuum.

Most extremophiles ("lovers of extremes") thrive on the tiny bacterial level. Microscopic tardigrades can tolerate radiation a thousand times greater than humans can, and they survive many years without water. Discoveries about extremophiles are giving astrobiologists a real boost as they change the parameters for looking for life forms in outer space. Could extreme "home sweet homes" be on icy comets? In the underground caves of other planets?

Tectonics: Shake It Up

In the second half of the twentieth century, some people were being urged to "go with the flow" when it came to handling stress. Turns out the earth had already been doing that for millions and billions of years— sort of. Scientists now think that the rigid upper layer of the earth, the lithosphere, has eight major tectonic plates and many more minor ones that move on top of the hotter, weaker, more mobile, more viscous asthenosphere.

Temperature differences, frictional drag, descending suction, and gravity all make the plate movements far from mellow when the edges meet, causing earthquakes, volcanoes, ocean trenches, and mountain-building.

Pangaea may be what the "earth" part of our planet looked like about 250 million years ago. Panthalassa ("all sea") is the ocean.

Mapmakers and explorers had previously speculated that the continents looked like puzzle pieces that once fit together. Geophysicist Alfred Wegener even suggested the Continental Drift Theory in 1912. It didn't prove entirely right, but it got people thinking. The name *Pangaea* ("all lands") was given to the single landmass that, around 250 million years ago, may have contained all of the continents. Decades later, scientists started establishing the dynamic notion of plate tectonics (Greek for "to build"), and the theory now unifies various earth sciences, including geology, seismology, and paleontology.

Oldie and Moldy: Antibiotics

The discovery of antibiotics (ancient Greek for "opposed to life") doesn't sound heartwarming, yet antibiotics have saved untold millions of people from dying, missing vacations, and generally feeling yucky.

The term *antibiotic* applies to microorganisms that can kill or retard the growth of harmful bacteria. German scientists were experimenting with antibiotics in the late-nineteenth and early-twentieth centuries, but the discovery that later saved lives is credited to a lucky Scotsman. Alexander Fleming accidentally "found" an antibiotic because he left his lab a mess, and a mold grew into penicillium, a fungus that can produce penicillin. For his discovery of what he called "mouldy juice," Fleming shared the Nobel Prize with Howard Florey and Ernst Chain, two diligent scientists who put the find into mass production in time to be "the wonder drug" for World War II.

Ancient Greeks, Egyptians, and Arabs all have records of using various molds to treat injuries and aid healing. Some ancients even put moldy bread right on the wounds. (If only they had been better at marketing.)

"I do not know what I may appear to the world; but to myself I seem to have been only like a boy playing on the seashore, and diverting myself in now and then finding a smoother pebble or a prettier shell than ordinary, whilst the great ocean of truth lay all undiscovered before me."

—Isaac Newton

Quirky Guys

Even before the current age of quarks*, there were men of science with amusing quirks. And even as they grappled with physics in serious life-and-death issues (such as bombs and fatal shuttle launches), the scientists had a humorous side.

Dirty Business

John von Neumann (1903–1957) made lasting contributions in computer architecture and science, quantum physics, meteorology, economics, game theory, and a long list of other fields. He may be best known for his pivotal work on the atom bomb at Los Alamos Labs.

He started off in Europe, managing to get degrees at universities in Heidelberg, Germany, and Zurich, Switzerland, at the same time. Then he moved to America, where he was invited to be one of the first faculty

*Quarks is the name given to tiny particles found in the protons and neutrons of the nuclei of atoms. The little whimsical eccentrics are challenging old views of physics with their unpredictable behavior.

members at the Institute of Advanced Studies at Princeton University. He developed a reputation for being a hard-core pragmatist and a hard-drinking party animal who collected and invented dirty jokes and limericks (most of which can't be printed in this book). He must have had quite a robust repertoire, since he'd started telling jokes in classical Greek as a kid.

You're Joking

Richard Feynman (1918–1988) was one of the best communicators of science in the twentieth century, but he didn't talk until he was three years old. He seemed to spend much of the rest of his life making up for his earlier silence, whether hitting his bongo drums as a deliberately and joyfully eccentric professor at the California Institute of Technology (Caltech), writing popular science books that made emerging new physics more accessible, or being the vital presidential panel member who explained in simple terms the scientific tragedy behind the Space Shuttle Challenger disaster.

While a junior research member of the Manhattan Project in Los Alamos, he got a bit bored, so he figured out how to guess the combinations and pick the locks of the high-security safes—and he left little notes in them. Oh yes, and while at Caltech, he was also known to use a topless bar as his off-campus office.

From Third to First Class

Perhaps the most space should go to a guy who changed and warped our view of space. He also didn't learn to talk until he was three years old. He failed his college entrance exams the first time, but did get a job as a patent officer—and a third-class one at that. He was even rejected when he applied to be a second-class patent officer. He wrote and published some scientific papers in 1905, then applied to be a lecturer at a university—and was rejected. He also failed to obtain a job teaching at a high school. Fortunately, he could still be a third-class patent examiner.

A "failure" who won the Nobel Prize.

You can thank Einstein for realizing: $E = mc^2$. This stands for: energy is equal to mass times the speed of light squared. The speed of light is 186,000 miles a second. Multiply that by itself and then by a mass (say, you), and that's a lot of energy!

After World War I, the world finally noticed the papers of **Albert Einstein** (1879–1955). His work changed the way we understand light, time, space, atoms, and energy. For one of these papers, he received the Nobel Prize, and he is deemed one of the greatest first-class minds of modern times. After working hard for peace, he left the dangers of Europe in 1933 and taught at Princeton University's Institute for Advanced Studies for many successful years.

Some of this genius's purported eccentricities included his purposely going sailing when there was no wind, just for the challenge of it; going sockless; and picking up cigarette butts off the ground (after his doctor told him to stop smoking his beloved pipe).

The Name Game at the Periodic Table

The Periodic Table of Elements is a well-organized chart of the most basic elements that make up our world. It's an essential aid in chemistry and a fascinating record of the advancement of science.

Some of the best minds throughout history were driven to uncover the elemental components of the universe. Many ancient Greeks thought there was a single element from which all else came, and they debated whether it was water, fire, or air. Anaximander concluded that everything was made from infinite amounts of an unknown substance called "apeirion."

We now know that there are many fundamental elements on earth. Air breaks down to oxygen and nitrogen, with a little carbon dioxide and argon. Water contains two atoms of hydrogen to one of oxygen. As scientists learned more about the basic building blocks, it became a challenge to organize the information about the elements by their chemical properties.

The Russian Dmitri Ivanovich Mendeleyev figured out the basis for the Periodic Table in 1869, possibly by making a card out of each element and playing a kind of solitaire. Elements are now organized horizontally in ascending order of their *atomic number* (the number of protons in the nucleus, which is the same as the number of electrons flitting about outside the nucleus). Hydrogen is one, helium two, and so on. All the elements in a row are considered to be in the same family with similar chemical characteristics, such as being gases or metals.

The names of many elements help mark trails of discovery that have furthered science over the years.

Mendelevium, with an atomic weight of 101, was named to memorialize the man who not only created the vertical and horizontal structure of the Periodic Table, but also correctly left blanks where he knew future elements had to be to complete patterns.

Rutherfordium honors the man who first split the nucleus of an atom and first figured out how to turn one kind of an atom into another. Ernest Rutherford used powerful alpha particles to turn nitrogen into oxygen in 1919.

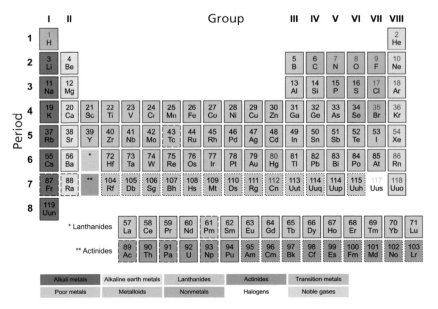

The Periodic Table of Elements.

Lawrencium recognizes the breakthroughs of Ernest Orlando Lawrence, who created the first cyclotron, or atom smasher, in 1931. The cyclotron—and later, more advanced accelerators—broke open a nucleus to add or create particles. These accelerators were a smashing success at discovering elements to fill the holes in the Periodic Table and to extend it. Most of these man-made elements have very short lives and are hard to reproduce.

Elements are often named by their discoverers but not after themselves. Many names show pride of place: **gallium** (Latin for France), **scandium** (Scandinavia), **germanium** (Germany), **americium**, and **californium**.

Research institutions also have their legacies in elements, such as **florentium** (University of Florence), **berkelium** (University of California, Berkeley), and **nobelium** (Nobel Institute in Sweden).

When Marie and Pierre Curie discovered an element, they named the element **polonium**, after Marie's homeland of Poland, instead of after her husband Pierre's country, France. One of Marie's students, though, Marguerite Perry, later found an element that she named **francium.**

Later, an element was named **curium** to honor the Curies. Other elements named to honor scientific giants include **einsteinium** (Albert Einstein) and **fermium** (Enrico Fermi). **Meitnerium** was named to honor Lise Meitner, a physicist who helped discover nuclear fission, but didn't want to work on the bomb at Los Alamos.

"Um"...Post–1800

After 1800, the custom was to end the names of all discovered metallic elements with "-ium" or "-um," and to end the names of all nonmetallic elements with "-on" or "-ine." **Chlorine, platinum, molybdenum,** and **tellurium** were found and named before 1800 but still follow the rule. There's only one exception. Take a look at the chart and make a guess.

Gold, silver, copper, iron, tin, lead, mercury, carbon, and **sulfur** were all known by the ancients. **Arsenic, antimony, bismuth,** and **zinc** were known before the end of the sixteenth century. **Nitrogen, oxygen,** and **hydrogen** were also all named before 1800.

It's the Law

In nature's legal system, scientific laws explain and mandate how the world works physically, and the laws aren't broken (that we know of). In fact, they were obeyed long before they were "discovered" and given names and mathematical formulas. These laws are so reliable they are also used to precisely predict many future outcomes.

Newton in Charge

Sir Isaac Newton delineated many of the laws, including the three **Laws of Motion**.

First Law a.k.a. The Law of Inertia: Things that aren't moving won't move unless acted upon. And things already moving will keep moving the same way unless acted upon.

Think of yourself sitting in a big comfy couch, and how you stay right where you are until something finally *makes* you move. Okay, your lungs are always moving as you breathe, but it could *look* like inertia. A better example would be a ball. Think of a ball "at rest." It's going to stay there for a long time until something acts on it—like you. If you push the ball, it would go forever if it weren't for friction, wind, obstacles, or other outside forces.

More formally put: "An object at rest will remain at rest unless acted on by an unbalanced force. An object in motion continues in motion with the same speed and in the same direction unless acted upon by an unbalanced force."

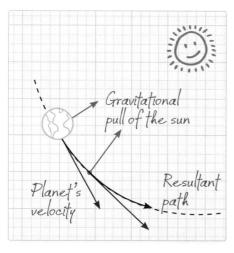

The sun's gravitational pull is one of the forces that keeps a planet in orbit, instead of continuing in a straight line.

Second Law: When a force acts on a mass, acceleration is produced. The bigger the mass (of what's being accelerated), the greater the force needed to make the object accelerate.

Newton's Second Law also gives us an exact relationship between force, mass, and acceleration. It can be expressed as a mathematical equation that isn't hard to remember:

$$Force = Mass \times Acceleration, \text{ or } f = ma$$

Reaction: balloon goes up

Action: air rushes down

Third Law: You've heard this one: For every action, there is an equal and opposite reaction. What does this mean? It's a kind of equality of forces.

For every force, there is a reaction force that is equal in size, but opposite in direction. If something pushes a separate object, it gets pushed back in the opposite direction equally as hard. Nature provides some simple examples: a bird pushes its wings down against the wind to go up, and a fish pushes its fins back against the water to go forward.

The Law of Orbits (a.k.a. Law of Ellipses)

One of the easiest laws to remember emerged a century before Newton's laws. The first of Johannes Kepler's three Laws of Planetary Motion, the Law of Orbits, was published in 1609. It states: "All planets move in elliptical orbits with the sun as the focus." Kepler's brilliant conclusions were based on the observations of the great Danish astronomer Tycho Brahe (before there was even a telescope).

The idea that planets orbit around the sun and moons orbit around planets in ellipses instead of perfect circles revolutionized ideas about the elegance of the cosmos.

Kepler also later coined the word "satellite," and his laws that describe "celestial mechanics" apply to all those modern-day satellites that keep television and the Internet going.

In Theory... Your Place in the Universe

Scientific theories are broad areas of understanding, supported by many given postulates and laws, and are generally accepted until proven incorrect either empirically or inductively.

The biggest theories seem to change previous views of Earth in the general scheme and scale of life. They are paradigm shifts that shake things up. Many of them are quite humbling to us as individuals, but quite grand in a broader perspective.

Heliocentrism

For over 1,500 years, Ptolemy's geocentric view of the universe was the stuff of mythologies, religions, and natural philosophy. He used plausible models

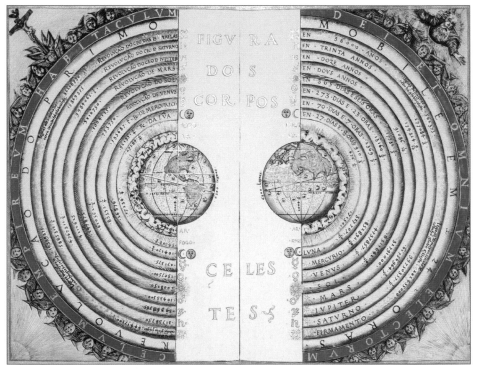

The planets orbit the earth in this geocentric illustration of Ptolemy's Universe by the Portuguese cartographer Bartolomeu Velho, published in his *Cosmographia*.

> *"The most exciting phrase to hear in science, the one that heralds the most discoveries, is not 'Eureka!' (I found it!) but 'That's funny . . .'"*
>
> —Isaac Asimov

and math (for what was known before the Common Era) to determine that Earth was right in the middle of *everything,* and that all other celestial objects revolved around it. Oops.

In 1543, however, Nicholas Copernicus published his *On the Revolutions of Celestial Spheres,* showing how the heavens above worked only if the *planets* revolved around the *sun* (not the Earth). This heliocentric view (*helio* is Greek for "sun"), or Copernican Revolution, helped kick off the Scientific Revolution of the sixteenth century. Instead of just accepting ancient Greek knowledge in medicine, astronomy, and other arenas as facts, more people started asking their own questions and conducting their own experiments.

Big Bang

As if heliocentrism weren't enough, it's now known that Earth is just one of billions of little orbiting orbs that fill the sky. From a cosmic perspective, Earth looks like an insignificant dot in our own Milky Way galaxy. The Big Bang Theory, which emerged in the late 1920s and early 1930s, says that the entire universe is in an expansive mode, having started very long ago with a very tiny compressed bit of matter (sometimes called a "singularity") that exploded into billions of galaxies and continues to expand.

Our planet is a tiny dot in the Milky Way, one galaxy among billions, in an expanding universe.

Guess who thought of this mind-exploding idea that known science is supporting? A Roman Catholic priest, Monsignor Lemaître from Belgium, applied Einstein's relativity rules and conceived of a "primeval atom" that started the whole universal shebang.

The US's Edwin Hubble also provided observations and solid math in the late 1920s and early 1930s that supported an expanding universe. Appropriately, the Hubble telescope named after him decades later gathered incredible images and data in recent years that show the universe to be receding from our little planet, confirming the idea that the universe is still expanding.

Albert Einstein considered it his "biggest blunder" that he sought a cosmic constant to support the idea of a *static* universe.

Theory of Evolution

Charles Darwin's Theory of Evolution, first published in *The Origin of Species* in 1859, basically says that life on Earth started as a single cell, and with the right conditions kept evolving via "natural selection" and "survival of the fittest." Traits that were good for survival survived while less effective traits were eliminated. The myriad results are a dazzling array of diversity adapted to different circumstances. According to the theory, pears, cats, whales, cactus, and humans are all related if you go back far enough. From day one, people of various religions refuted the notion, and now with the latest findings on the tiniest levels, new questions are being raised.

An "All" Theory

Scientists are still searching for the GUT (General Unified Theory) or TOE (Theory of Everything) that will unify Einstein's Theory of Relativity and James Clarke Maxwell's theories on electromagnetism together with what scientists know about the weak and strong interactions between particles that cause radiation, nuclear reactions, and other physical phenomena.

"Every discovery opens a new field for investigation of facts, shows us the imperfection of our theories. It has justly been said, that the greater the circle of light, the greater the boundary of darkness by which it is surrounded."

—Sir Humphry Davy

String Theory

Small one-dimensional parts of particles called *strings* are central in the relatively new String Theory, which has been developing over the last three decades. What if strings' vibrations at different frequencies create different forces? Of course, it's not quite that simple, but it is fascinating and scientists are currently exploring new mathematics and views of physics, including the idea that we live in a world with at least eleven dimensions.

Science is far from being a static body of knowledge to learn. Some of the greatest adventures start with the questions that arise from new answers.

The Spin on the Oceans

"Earth" is a bit of a misnomer for our planet when you consider that over seventy-three percent of the surface is water, and the average depth of the oceans is over two miles. So it makes sense, then, that oceanography is an important branch of science and deserves serious attention—and some spin. When you look at an ocean map of big gyres (rotating ocean currents), it looks like the equator is a dividing line for spin. These massive gyres can have great impact on creature ecologies, human trash in the

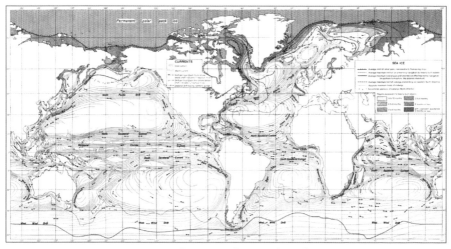

Ocean Currents and Sea Ice from Atlas of World Maps,
United States Army Service Forces, Army Specialized Training Division.
Army Service Forces Manual M-101 (1943).

oceans, navigation, the weather, and more.

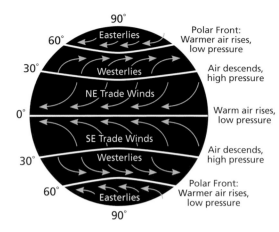

Moving clouds and ocean currents appear mostly clockwise above the equatorial line and counterclockwise below it, so it appears there's spin to the right in the Northern Hemisphere and spin to the left in the Southern Hemisphere. Welcome to the **Coriolis Effect**.

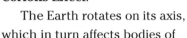

Global circulation of Earth's atmosphere.

The Earth rotates on its axis, which in turn affects bodies of water and clouds, and literally puts a spin on Newton's laws of motion. When you look at motion from a "rotational frame of reference," not an "inertial" one, you have to factor in centrifugal force and deflection velocities, and other scientific factors that mean, well, things look different for the top and bottom halves of the globe. A man named Gaspard-Gustav Coriolis helped figure it out in mathematical terms that might make your head spin too.

For a simple insight, though, **here's something to try at home**. Grab a large orange (or apple, if you like Newton) and think of it as Earth. Take your finger and make a clockwise circular motion on the top of the orange as you look at it from above. Keep your finger circling the same way, but raise the orange above your eyes—suddenly the *same* circular motion seems to be counterclockwise!

In the actual oceans, some factors that enhance or disrupt the spin of ocean currents include landmasses, the dominating winds, temperature, salinity, lunar tides, proximity to the poles, and high and low pressure systems that impact movement.

Various factors also mean the Coriolis Effect is a bit of an urban-plumbing myth when it comes to watching bathtubs drain and toilets flush in the opposite hemisphere. There are more powerful factors, like the direction in which the water is released, and the angle at which the water hits the porcelain. You don't have to book a ticket to Australia to see water spinning counter-clockwise down the drain. It may or may not happen in your own home regardless of what latitude you live in.

Extra Credit

Have the tidbits about great discoveries, unbreakable laws, and unanswered questions prompted you to want to learn more? Have the teasers about oceanography, astronomy, and chemistry catalyzed you to dive in, look up, or play with the elements? Then gold stars for you! You already have the curiosity of a scientist!

For those of you who like prompts and review, pick any or all of the three below:

1) Go outside tonight and find the North Star, then jump up to see if gravity still works.

2) Close your eyes and try to visualize a world with more than four dimensions.

3) Think about your friends. Are they more like extremophiles or neuroecologists? Singularities or satellites? Cyclotrons, comets, or continental drift? Meteorites or meteors? Quarks or quirks? Are their exponential powers more like yotta or yocto?

For those who want to search for extra credit, which science quote in the chapter do you like best? Asimov's? Dewey's? Davy's? Newton's? Why?

Who Are You?

Where do you fit into life on Earth? Are you an Annelid like an earthworm, an Echinoderm like a starfish, a Chordate like a frog, or an Arthropod like a dragonfly? See page 140 for the answer.

Philosophy & Religion 101

WHY DO YOU BELIEVE WHAT YOU BELIEVE? WHAT TENETS DO YOU LIVE by? What do you consider right and wrong? What are your goals in life? Do you believe in an afterlife? Why do we exist? What is truth? Faith? Reality?

Philosophy and religions have been supplying questions and answers about our existence and values since before written records existed. You could say that philosophy (meaning "the love of wisdom" in Greek) engages the mind on these quests, and religion the heart and soul, but it's not quite that simple.

Philosophy also delves into issues of the soul and heart, and religion also involves the mind. Whether you have a firm position or are seeking one, and whether you justify your stance with philosophical arguments or take it on faith, this chapter may add some answers *and* some questions to your life.

Religion
Sacred Places

All over the globe, there are places considered sacred by believers. People have plotted migrations to divine destinations throughout the millennia. To this day, humans continue to make pilgrimages to places of prayer. Millions of Hindus, for example, travel every year to their holy site in the city of Varanasi, on the banks of the Ganges River in Uttar Pradesh, India. The Vatican in Rome draws Catholics from all over the world, and the Temple in Salt Lake City, Utah, attracts Mormons. Buddhists travel to a different temple—the Mahabodhi Temple in Bodhgaya, India—where it's believed the Buddha attained enlightenment under a tree. The aborigines in Australia have made pilgrimages

to their sacred Uluru (Ayers Rock) for thousands of years. Worldwide, people continue to visit new religious spots, honor ongoing sacred places, and uncover ancient sites of worship.

Chichén Itzá   *Göbekli Tepe*   *Mount Fuji*

Cave of Machpelah   *The Holy Mosque in Mecca*

Göbekli Tepe, rediscovered in the twenty-first century in southern Turkey near the Syrian border, is thousands of years older than Stonehenge, and it may be the oldest known temple site. German and Turkish archeologists unearthed T-shaped pillars and monoliths with animal carvings and the sacred symbols of a Neolithic hunter-gatherer people, who were mostly nomads. Preliminary findings indicate that this was a center of worship for visitors before the invention of either the wheel or agriculture.

Mount Fuji, or Fujiyama, was sacred to the aboriginal people of Japan, and the name of the volcano honors their fire goddess, Fuchi. In the Shinto religion, Mount Fuji is a portal to another world. A shrine to the goddess of the mountain, Sengen-Sama, sits on the summit. Each year, millions climb to the top of Japan's tallest and holiest mountain to honor the rising sun.

Tombs of the Patriarchs (Cave of Machpelah) have been revered for thousands of years as the believed burial site of Abraham, Isaac, Jacob, and their wives. The site, located in Hebron in the West Bank, is holy to the

Jewish, Christian, and Islamic faiths, which all consider Abraham to be a prophet. The multiple claims on the site caused conflict during the medieval crusades and the modern era. Since Herod added structures in the first century BCE, mosques, a cathedral, a synagogue, and military forts have all been built there at various times.

Chichén Itzá, in the Yucatán peninsula of Mexico, draws tourists from around the world today, but from about the middle of the sixth century, the ceremonial site attracted indigenous travelers and pilgrims. The Mayan architecture and later Toltec structures include temples, sacrificial altars, a pyramid, and a ball court the size of a football stadium. Other highlights include a large *cenote* (a sinkhole of groundwater or natural well), once a sacred place for sacrifices, and El Caracol, a Mayan observatory with a spiral staircase and windows carved to frame certain stars and planets at particular times. Astronomy was part of the Mayan religion, interrelated with rituals and ceremonies.

The Holy Mosque in Mecca is the sacred destination for Muslims. Five times a day, Muslims all over the world turn toward Mecca (a.k.a. Makkah) in Saudi Arabia and pray. There, the world's largest Muslim mosque, Masjid al-Haram, surrounds the ancient quasi-cubical Ka'aba with the revered Black Stone that Islamic tradition says has links to Adam and Eve, Abraham, and Mohammed. It is said that at the Ka'aba, Mohammed kissed the Black Stone and had hundreds of tribal idols destroyed, declaring the Ka'aba a shrine again for the monotheistic faith of Islam. Devout Muslims hope to make a Mecca pilgrimage (Hajj) to the Holy Mosque at least once in a lifetime, and walk seven times around the gathering spot of the Ka'aba.

{ **fyi** }

In animism, one of the oldest belief systems, people, animals, trees, rocks, waterfalls, and other aspects of nature are believed to have souls or spirits. Animists may encounter any number of sacred places on a walk through a forest.

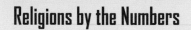

Religions by the Numbers

Worldwide

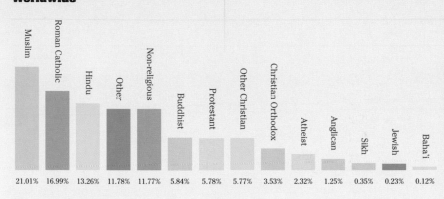

Muslim	Roman Catholic	Hindu	Other	Non-religious	Buddhist	Protestant	Other Christian	Christian Orthodox	Atheist	Anglican	Sikh	Jewish	Baha'i
21.01%	16.99%	13.26%	11.78%	11.77%	5.84%	5.78%	5.77%	3.53%	2.32%	1.25%	0.35%	0.23%	0.12%

United States

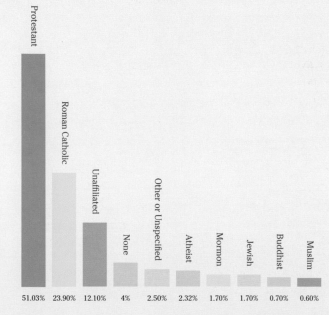

Protestant	Roman Catholic	Unaffiliated	None	Other or Unspecified	Atheist	Mormon	Jewish	Buddhist	Muslim
51.03%	23.90%	12.10%	4%	2.50%	2.32%	1.70%	1.70%	0.70%	0.60%

Source: The World Factbook 2009. Washington, DC: Central Intelligence Agency, 2009.

Holy Texts and Teachings

Most religions have words or texts deemed holy, whether they are considered open to interpretation or held to be absolute in meaning. For many indigenous spiritual cultures, these guiding words were passed on orally through time. Some of the great sacred texts started as oral teachings and were later written down; most are believed to have been divinely dictated or revealed. These books have changed lives through the centuries and are still revered as sacred by billions.

HINDUISM

The Vedas, containing hymns, chants, and rituals, are among the oldest spiritual texts known to exist. Written in Sanskrit, they are considered the holy books for Hindus, but also influenced the development of later religions, including Buddhism, Sikhism, and Jainism. The oldest of the four Vedas, the Rig Veda, was verbally transmitted as early as 1500 BC. The other three Vedas—Sama Veda, Yajur Veda, and Atharva Veda—are also considered to be core Hindu spiritual texts.

The Upanishads, written later and over many hundreds of years, include writings about the importance of karma—the spiritual sum-effects of one's actions—and discuss the importance of meditation in bringing the soul and truth together.

The Bhagavad Gita, written between the fifth and second centuries BCE, is a good introduction to Hindu philosophy and the Vedas because the basic truths are explained in a discussion between Krishna and Arjuna before a key battle.

Hindus are often characterized by a connection to the sacred writings of the Vedic books. Unlike other major faiths, Hinduism doesn't have a single founder, catalyzing historic event, or a central religious organization. From prehistoric to current times, many religious sects, practices, and schools of Hinduism with varying beliefs have evolved. Hinduism has even been called monotheistic (worshipping one deity) by some and polytheistic (worshipping many divinities) by others. Generally, though, as expressed in their holy texts, Hindus believe in an everlasting soul and reincarnation; in the importance of Brahma, Vishnu, and Shiva, the God trinity; and that the soul can be freed via duty, knowledge, and devotion.

{ **fyi** }

Most of the more than one billion Hindus alive today live in India, but Hinduism's influence has spread across the globe. For example, yoga, ayurvedic health, karma, and chakras all have roots in the ancient Vedas.

JUDAISM

The Jewish Bible, called the *Tanakh* in Hebrew, is the core spiritual book for Judaism as well as the source of the Old Testament of the later Christian religions, and parts of the even-later Islam faith. It was written in Biblical Hebrew (from right to left, without vowels).

A Hebrew version, called the Masoretic Text, emerged during the seventh to tenth centuries with information on how to pronounce and read the works. The Tanakh contains three parts:

The Torah (Pentateuch), the "five books of Moses," is believed by many to have been written by Moses, who was divinely inspired by "the one and only God," referred to as Yahweh. The five books are known in English as Genesis, Exodus, Leviticus, Numbers, and Deuteronomy.

The Prophets (*Nevi'im*) cover, not surprisingly, the era of prophets from the time the Jewish people entered the Promised Land, or the Land of Canaan, to the time the Jews were expelled by King Nebuchadnezzar II, around 600 BCE. (That's more than 2,600 years ago!)

The Writings (*Ketuvim*), or Scriptures, contain the books of truth, wisdom, poetry, and history, including Psalms, Proverbs, Ecclesiastes, Chronicles, and more.

The Talmud, an essential collection of rabbinical discussions on Jewish law, history, and culture, also explains much of the content of the *Tanakh*. It was was gathered from older sources in the middle of the fifth century BCE and organized by 120 sages, scribes, and prophets of the Great Assembly.

CHRISTIANITY

The Christian Bible is the central religious text and holy scriptures of Christian religions. The work is divided in two main sections: the Old Testament and the New Testament.

Translated from the Tanakh, the books of the **Old Testament** focus on the creation of the Earth, and the relations between God and man before the birth of Jesus of Nazareth, also known as Jesus Christ. **The Apocrypha** are books that are included in various versions of the Old Testament in Catholic and Orthodox Bibles; but they are not deemed to be Holy Scripture to Protestants, so were left out of their editions.

The New Testament, written later by many authors, presents a new covenant with God and tells of the teachings and life of Christ, including his birth, life, death, and resurrection. It includes the Gospels of Matthew, Mark, Luke, and John.

Various Christian faiths have versions of the Bible they believe to be divinely inspired. In each, the books or chapters have different names, numbers, and order. Key translations include the Vulgate, a Latin version used by the Catholic Church for centuries; a German version translated by Martin Luther and called the Geneva Bible; and an English version called the King James Bible. If it's all Greek to you, you may be reading the Septuagint version of the Old Testament—the oldest translation from Hebrew to Greek, made in about the third century BCE.

ISLAM

The Qur'an (or Koran) is the main holy book of Islam, the religion practiced by Muslims (translated as "one who submits to God"). Muslims believe the book to be the direct and most recent word of "the one and only God," called Allah, and the scriptures are believed to have been revealed to Mohammed through the angel Gabriel, from the year 610 until Mohammed's death in 632 CE (or 10 AH—see the **fyi** on the next page).

Mohammed memorized those revelations and recited them to followers as he served as the chosen prophet, political leader, and military commander, uniting the fractious Arabic tribes as one. The messages were codified and written down, in Arabic, after his death. Muslims believe they contain revelations from Allah going back to the first Muslim prophet,

{ **fyi** }

Islamic calendars and timelines are based not on the birth of Jesus, but on the day Mohammed and his followers left Mecca for what is now Medina (about 622 CE), in a migration called the Hijra. The year 2011 on the Julian or Western calendar would be approximately 1432 AH (After Hijra, or Anno Hegirae in Latin).

Adam, and are the truest word from God, correcting prior corruptions in the monotheistic faith that extended through prophets from Adam, Abraham, Moses, and Jesus to Mohammed.

The Qur'an offers guidance for righteous living and consists of 114 *suras*, or chapters; but they do not form a linear narrative with a beginning, middle, and end. Each chapter, except number nine, begins with "Basmala" or "Bismillah," an Islamic noun that stands for the phrase "In the name of God, most Gracious, most Merciful." The ninth chapter is sometimes known as "The Repentance" or "The Ultimatum."

The Sufi, Sunni, and Shia are different branches of the Muslim faith, and they interpret the verses of the Qur'an differently.

BUDDHISM

Some consider Buddhism a religion; others call it a philosophy. Buddhism is not based on divine revelation, absolute scriptures, or intermediaries between individuals and the divine. Buddhism suggests that one can be guided by another's teachings *and* one's own experiences.

The founding teacher was Siddhartha Gautama, a.k.a. the Buddha, a Sanskrit word meaning "Awakened One." He enjoyed palatial pampering in his early life, then sought an acetic life of suffering for spiritual growth, and finally determined that a "Middle Way"—neither overindulgence nor extreme deprivation—was the best path to enlightenment. Buddhist beliefs recommend the Four Noble Truths and the Noble Eightfold Path.

Four Noble Truths
- Existence is full of suffering
- Suffering results from desire and ignorance
- Craving and attachment (desire) can be eliminated
- The Buddhist Eightfold Path can lead to Nirvana (no desire)

Noble Eightfold Path
- Right understanding/view
- Right thought/intention
- Right speech
- Right action
- Right livelihood
- Right effort
- Right mindfulness
- Right concentration

Like other major faiths, Buddhism has different branches, schools, denominations, and sects within it. Two of the most vital branches are Mahayana Buddhism, which is found mostly in Northern Asia—Japan, China, Mongolia, Tibet—and Theravada Buddhism, which is found mostly in Southern Asia—Sri Lanka, Cambodia, Burma, Thailand.

Theravada Buddhism is based largely on Gautama Buddha and previous teachings, and Mahayana follows the Gautama Buddha and subsequent teachings. Sects of Mahayana include Zen, Pure Land, and certain yogic systems.

Philosophy
The Major Branches of Philosophy

Socrates taught Plato, who, in turn, taught Aristotle, several centuries before the birth of Jesus. Discarding the mantle of mythology, and using the mind and senses of man, they sought defendable answers to the great questions that we still pursue today as lovers of wisdom. The key areas of inquiry include:

Metaphysics, or "beyond the physical," studies realities not explained by known facts. "Is there a God? Why are we here?"

Epistemology is the study of knowledge and includes rationalism and empiricism. "How do I know I exist? What is knowledge?"

Ethics concerns moral values—right and wrong, good and evil—and ethical concerns, including the death penalty, abortion, and euthanasia. "Who decides what is objectively moral? How should we act?"

Logic is a methodology for clear thinking and can help in the study of all branches of philosophy. (Think Spock from *Star Trek*.) "What is the correct reasoning for things?"

Aesthetics is the study of beauty and art. "What roles do our senses, emotions, and intellect play in perceiving the world? How do we judge nature and culture?"

Some Related Reading from Western Texts

Metaphysics: Aristotle's *Metaphysics*, Spinoza's *Ethics*, and Leibniz's *Theodicy*

Epistemology: Descartes' *Meditations on First Philosophy*, Kant's *Critique of Pure Reason*, Hume's *Treatise on Human Nature*, Locke's *An Essay Concerning Human Understanding*, Russell's *Problems of Philosophy*

Ethics: Aristotle's *Nicomachean Ethics*, Kant's *Grounding for the Metaphysic of Morals*, chapter two of John Stuart Mill's *Utilitarianism*

Logic: Aristotle's *Prior and Posterior Analytics and Organon*, Bertrand Russell and Alfred North Whitehead's *Principia Mathematica*

Aesthetics: Aristotle's *Rhetoric and Poetics*, Kant's *Critique of Judgment*, Kant's lectures

Ponder These Philosophers

Lucius Annaeus Seneca, a.k.a. Seneca or Seneca the Younger (4 BCE–65 CE), preached self-discipline and restraint as a Stoic, but he carried on multiple sexual affairs and lived sensually—or, so say his critics. Some historians, however, think the besmirchers of his reputation may have been motivated by jealousy of the very talented playwright and philosopher.

Seneca's death seemed even less fair. He was a cogent Roman sage and tutor to Emperor Nero for years, but was ordered to commit suicide, because Nero thought he was a spy and part of a plot to kill the Emperor.

"Difficulties strengthen the mind, as labor the body," is a popular quote attributed to Seneca. His mandated suicide was quite difficult. One report says he slit his wrists, then his legs, and still didn't die. Poison was slow too. So, at last, he got in a tub of hot water and, in a weakened state, was asphyxiated by the steam.

Bishop Berkeley (pronounced *BAR*-klee) (1685–1753) was an Irish philosopher with an eclectic life. He contributed to the field of optics, wrote a poem that inspired the naming of the University of California, Berkeley (pronounced *BUR*-klee), set up a center in Bermuda to train missionaries for the colonies and native inhabitants, pointed out weaknesses in calculus, and developed "immaterialism" philosophy, positing that things exist only because they are perceived. He wrote several books in his lifetime, including *A Treatise Concerning the Principles of Human Knowledge*, which is still read today. His most popular book during his own life, though, concerned the value of using tar water as an antiseptic and as a general cure for disease.

Immanuel Kant (1724–1804) was a German philosopher, mathematician, and scientist with a far-reaching impact in the world, yet he never traveled more than a hundred miles from his home in his whole life. He was born in Königsberg*, Prussia, attended the University of Königsberg, taught at the university, and died there.

Kant's insights helped expand astronomy past the study of our solar system, and his thinking influenced key brains from Karl Marx to Albert

{ **fyi** }

Königsberg became Kaliningrad, Russia, in World War II, and in 2005, Kant's alma mater, the University of Königsberg, was renamed the Immanuel Kant State University of Russia. Kalingrad is now bordered by Lithuania and Poland, but is considered part of Russia.

*See page 60 for a puzzle about the bridges of Königsberg. Although it was an inland city, it was also a river city.

Einstein. His books, including *Critique of Pure Reason*, are considered seminal works that changed the course of philosophy. Even though he spent his entire life in an inland city, he was the first to note that tidal currents affect the speed of the Earth's rotation.

Arthur Schopenhauer (1788–1860) viewed fellow German philosopher G. W. F. Hegel (1770–1831) as an unworthy rival. In 1820, Schopenhauer taught a class at the University of Berlin at the same time Hegel did. When more students showed up for Hegel's class than for his, Schopenhauer said "*auf wiedersehen*" (goodbye) to college life.

Eleven years later, when cholera struck in 1831, both philosophers left Berlin to be safe. Hegel returned to his university post to teach students in the fall, and he died in November. Schopenhauer, on the other hand, moved south, and lived. For almost three decades, he dwelled alone, it is said, except for a series of pet poodles named either Butz or Atma.

Schopenhauer's main work, *The World as Will and Representation*, presents a philosophy similar to Buddhism. To vastly oversimplify, he argued that human desires and motivations (what he called "will") can't be fulfilled, and therefore it is better to live without them.

Søren Kierkegaard (1813–1855), a great Danish thinker, wrote a university thesis called *On the Concept of Irony with Continual References to Socrates*. It involved three years of scholarship and was considered to be good, but too witty for a solemn academic work.

Kierkegaard once wrote, "Once you label me, you negate me," but he nevertheless has become regarded as "the father of existentialism." His books include *Either/Or*, *Fear and Trembling*, and *The Sickness Unto Death*. He used parody, satire, irony, dialectics, and polemics in his writings to engage the reader in reflection and passion, believing that how one chooses to live is the ultimate personal truth.

He also said, "Life can only be understood backwards; but it must be lived forwards." Appropriately, his influence was felt more after he died.

Extra Credit

Pascal's Wager

Blaise Pascal (1623–1662), a brilliant Frenchmen, was writing original mathematical proofs at age eleven and grew up to contribute significantly to mathematics and science. He also is credited with inventing a type of syringe, as well as early calculators.

After being in a near-fatal carriage accident when he was thirty-one, Pascal had a mystical vision. He decided to put science aside and devote himself to theology and philosophy. His controversial book, *Provincial Letters,* written under a pseudonym, was both hailed as great French literature and ordered to be burned by Louis XIV. Pope Alexander publicly disapproved of the book but began reforms in the Catholic Church, possibly because of it.

In note 233 of his next book, *Pensées*, Pascal posited that even though God's existence cannot be proven through reason, a person would do better to live life as though God exists—one would have everything to gain (if there is, in fact, a God) and nothing to lose (if there turns out to be no God). *Pensées* was a posthumously published collection of notes made in Pascal's last years, as he worked on a treatise on rational arguments supporting the Christian faith.

This argument, "Pascal's Wager," has been debated through the centuries and credited with contributing to the later fields of decision theory, probability theory, and the philosophies of volunteerism and pragmatism.

About six centuries earlier, Imam al-Haramayn al-Juwayni had written a version of this "wager" for the Islamic faith in his *Guide to the Conclusive Proofs for the Principles of Belief*. And there's an even older version of the wager in Sanskrit in the *Pram'na-samuccaya* (*A Compendium of Validities*) by

Dign'ga (480–540 CE). It's translated roughly as "If there is no life after death, then there is nothing to fear either way; but if there is, then it will be the atheists who will stand to suffer."

What's your bet? Your five-hundred-word essay need not be in French, Arabic, or Sanskrit.

Blaise Pascal (1623–1662) studying the cycloid, engraved on the tablet. The scattered papers at his feet are his *Pensées*, the open book is his *Lettres Provinciales*.

Bonus Chapter: Psychology 101

Are you an eclectic braniac with all your newfound 101 knowledge of astronomy, economics, and fun vocabulary words? If so, you can thank your brain! If you want to keep learning and improving your life, you might also want to give your brain some *extra* help. That's why there's this little *extra* bonus chapter.

Humans don't have wings or flippers or tails. Our senses of sight and smell and hearing aren't nearly as keen as many other animals' either, but we do have fantastically complex brains that help us function, innovate, and adapt. Our brains and our roughly one hundred billion neuron communicators, or nerve cells, help us take in the world and interpret it and make choices.

Psychology, the scientific study of the mind and behavior, can help you understand yourself and the others around you better. The term *psycho* has gotten a bad wrap (as in "psychopath"), but psychology is not just about studying mental illness and pathologies. *Psycho* is Greek for "spirit," "soul," and "mind." Here are some peeks at what psychology is investigating about personality, behavior, and intelligence, and some tips on how to better learn everything else.

"The unexamined life is not worth living." —Socrates

What's Your Personality?

You may already feel well acquainted with your own ticks, traits, and talents, but taking personality evaluations can give you insights or prompt instructive reactions. Like intelligence tests, personality tests, including the MBTI and FFM (keep reading!), are just indicators, not prescriptions or predictors.

Meyers-Briggs Type Indicator (MBTI)

The MBTI, or "instrument," as it is called, is a psychometric tool designed to help people learn what personality type they are and how they make decisions. Katherine Briggs and her daughter Isabel Briggs Myers developed the Myers-Briggs Type Indicator tool in the 1940s, based on C. G. Jung's work on psychological types from the 1920s. It started as an idea to help women entering the WWII workforce match well with a suitable job, but it has grown into an industry of its own for men and women.

The MBTI is purported to determine sixteen basic personality types based on four parameters:

ENFJ seeking ESTJ. Please have MBTI results handy.

- Whether you are Extraverted (E) or Introverted (I)
- Whether you rely on Sensing (S) or Intuition (N) for information
- Whether you are Thinking (T) or Feeling (F) in the way you approach a situation
- Whether you are Judging (J) or Perceiving (P) in how you make decisions

After taking a multiple-choice questionnaire, you are given a four-letter personality type (for example, an "ESTJ" or an "INFP"), along with a trained professional's assessment and guidance.

The Big Five

Another personality test is known as the Five Factor Model (FFM). You are asked to rate certain statements (such as "I like to meet new people") from "highly agree" to "highly disagree."

You are then told how you rank in five areas, which can be abbreviated as OCEAN:

- Openness to experiences
- Conscientiousness
- Extraversion
- Agreeableness
- Neuroticism

The Extraordinary You

Leading psychologist Dr. Howard Gardner and his associates at Harvard University have spent years studying the characteristics that extraordinary people—like Gandhi and Mozart—share. They've also culled activities that less-renowned people can practice to add some "extra" to the ordinary.

- Reflect: Regularly set aside time to think about your day-to-day life and how it fits in with your longer-term aims.
- Frame: Frame your setbacks in a way that lets you learn from them, so future actions can be better. Like photographs, our experiences can look different, depending on how we frame them.
- Leverage: Know your strengths and make the best use of them. Maximize the best of your unique combination of assets.

Behavior Experiments

How much of your behavior is your character and personality, and how much is influenced by the situation you are in? How much is nature and how much is nurture? Psychologists often create experiments to gain insights. The results of some famous ones aren't always pretty.

Prison Break

The **Zimbardo Prison Experiment** at Stanford University in 1971 studied the psychology of captivity. Psychologists created a mock prison, and student participants were randomly assigned the roles of prisoners or guards. After six days of an intended two-week experiment, Professor Phillip Zimbardo shut down the exercise when some of the "guards" manifested sadism, and some of the previously healthy "inmates" began suffering psychological disorders. The students' alarming intensities in their roles were interpreted as support for the idea of *situational behavior*, rather than *dispositional character*.

More Pain, Please

In the earlier, somewhat infamous **Miligram experiments**, Yale psychologist Stanley Miligram tested people's reactions to authority figures, in part to explore whether the atrocities committed during World War II could have been done under the guise of "just following orders." In a series of experiments started in 1961, participants were asked to push a buzzer to increase the amount of pain given to a subject. (They didn't know that the subjects were planted and the pain was faked.) The results were startling. In a choice between following the authority or following one's own moral beliefs against inflicting pain, the authority usually won. The button was pushed, sometimes even while the victims were screaming.

Not all experiments are so extreme. Some of the classic ones provide more welcome insights.

Dog Drool

What do you think of when you hear of **Pavlov's dogs**? Slobber? If you salivate every time you are about to receive your favorite treat, you understand this experiment. The Russian physician and psychologist Ivan Petrovich Pavlov received the Nobel Prize in Medicine in 1904 for his research on mammals' digestive systems—but you may know him best because of dog drool. In his experiments intended to research the chemistry of dogs' saliva in reaction to different foods, Pavlov noticed that the dogs salivated *before* they ate or were even served food, in reflexive reactions to certain cues. He switched his focus and discovered what he called "conditional reflexes," a.k.a. conditioned responses.

Kinds of Intelligences
Multiple Intelligences Theory

For many years, academics and IQ (Intelligence Quotient) tests were based largely on people's linguistic, logical, and mathematical strengths—their pen-and-paper prowess. In 1983, however, Dr. Howard Gardner introduced a theory that everyone had multiple intelligences in varying degrees. His original Multiple Intelligences (MI) Theory focused on seven kinds of intelligences in life:

- Linguistic
- Logical/Mathematical
- Bodily/Kinesthetic
- Musical

- Spatial
- Interpersonal
- Intrapersonal

In the late 1990s, an eighth intelligence was added:

- Naturalistic

Gardner showed that there are many ways to learn new material, comprehend concepts, and be "smart" in life besides the abilities that help you get a high score on an IQ test. You may be better able to learn through communicating with others, or through introspection, the natural world, or music. Different strengths support different kinds of careers and various kinds of learning. MI is now used by hundreds of schools throughout the world. Here's a simple example: Some people may really understand how the electrons go around the nucleus of an atom by reading about it; others may want to see a three-dimensional model; some may benefit most by physically acting out the parts and racing around the designated nucleus like an electron; some may want to work in a cooperative group to create a project about an atom, while still others may learn best by making up a song about it.

Triarchic Theory of Intelligence

Psychologist Robert Sternberg developed a different theory of intelligence while he was a Professor of Psychology and Education at Yale. In 1985 he proposed that "successful intelligence" combines three different strands:

- Analytical intelligence, which refers to problem-solving abilities
- Creative intelligence, which involves the ability to deal with new situations using past experiences and current skills
- Practical intelligence, which refers to the ability to adapt to a changing environment

Best-selling Intelligences

Dr. Daniel Goleman, a science journalist and renowned psychologist, has also challenged the previous views of IQ and proposed alternatives in his popular books that speak to current times. His book *Emotional Intelligence* (1996) has sold over five million copies and his *Ecological Intelligence* (2009) is a twenty-first century way of looking at intelligence in the world.

- Emotional Intelligence (EI), Goleman says, is more important than the standard-tested IQ for success and survival in the workplace and in life. Empathy, self-motivation, strong listening skills, mastery over our impulses, and the ability to resolve conflicts are all important to use and cultivate.

- Social Intelligence (SI) is an innate part of being human. Emerging brain research and new findings in biology show that people are "hardwired" to connect to others.
- Ecological Intelligence is how we interconnect with nature and the ecologies that humans have built, as well as how we make the choices we do and their subsequent impact on the planet.

Smart Parts to Help You Learn

The brain is a marvelously complex center with diverse parts that serve various functions. For a quick take on the sections that scientists think help you learn, here are some smart parts to remember:

- **Prefrontal cortex** is for thought and problem solving
- **Broca's area** is for speech
- **Wernicke's area** is for language comprehension

Our key cortexes for the senses that help learning include:

- **Primary somatosensory cortex** is the receptive area for your sense of touch
- **Primary auditory cortex** is for processing sound information
- **Primary visual cortex** is for receiving visual input from the retina

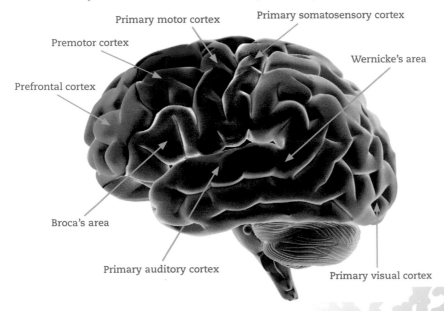

Primary motor cortex

Primary somatosensory cortex

Premotor cortex

Wernicke's area

Prefrontal cortex

Broca's area

Primary auditory cortex

Primary visual cortex

Smarten Up for Everything!

Learn more. Learning begets learning. The more you learn, the more nerve cell connectors will grow, giving you much more smart-potential.

Add ZZZs for As. Studies show that sleep is essential for good brain function and processing. A short siesta can also boost learning results, but power naps should augment, not replace, a good night's sleep.

Know your best learning styles. Figure out whether you learn better when you hear something, see it, or write it down. Then support yourself in your pursuit of knowledge. If hearing things makes them stick better for you, find a podcast on the subject or record your own voice reading passages from a textbook. Play on your strengths, whatever your dominant intelligences are.

Breathe for the brain. Exercise promotes oxygen flow to the brain. People with good aerobic health have proven to do better on mental tests. Deep breathing can also increase oxygen flow and fan some thinking-fire in your brain.

Forgo drugs and alcohol. Whether your response to that is "duh" or "oh, no!" the evidence shows that drugs and alcohol do *not* help memory. Quite the contrary.

Subtract stress. Whether your response mode is fight-or-flight, veg out or freak out, your neural networks are not performing at optimal learning capacity when you are overly stressed. Music helps some people relax and retain more of what they've learned.

Reread this book. What more is there to say?

Best wishes for your Life 101!

"To thine own self be true." —William Shakespeare

Answers

History 101

Seven Ancient Wonders

1) Great Pyramid of Giza (the only one of the ancient seven wonders that is still standing)
2) Hanging Gardens of Babylon
3) Statue of Zeus at Olympia
4) Temple of Artemis at Ephesus
5) The Tomb of Maussollus (or Mausoleum) at Halicarnassus
6) Colossus of Rhodes
7) Lighthouse of Alexandria

Literature & Grammar 101

Female or Male?

Eudora Welty: FEMALE (Eudora Alice Welty) Pulitzer Prize–winning Southern novelist (*The Optimist's Daughter*) and short story writer. The email program Eudora was named after her.

Ezra Pound: MALE (Edward Weston Loomis Pound) Poet (*The Cantos*) who helped the careers of his contemporaries, including Robert Frost, William Carlos Williams, and Marianne Moore.

Flannery O'Connor: FEMALE (Mary Flannery O'Connor) Another influential Southern writer (*A Good Man Is Hard to Find*) and critic.

George Eliot: FEMALE (Mary Ann Evans) Author of *Middlemarch* and *Silas Marner*. In her lifetime, her novels were more popular than those of Jane Austen, who died a couple of years before Eliot was born.

George Sand: FEMALE (born Amandine Aurore Lucile Dupin, but later became Baroness Dudevant) Novelist and playwright. She wrote *A Winter in Majorca* about her time spent with composer Frederic Chopin.

Harper Lee: FEMALE (Nelle Harper Lee) Author of *To Kill a Mockingbird*. She and neighbor Truman Capote (*In Cold Blood*) enjoyed writing together on her Underwood typewriter when they were children.

Word Wisdom

1. H	6. B
2. E	7. C
3. J	8. D
4. F	9. A
5. I	10. G

Bonus answer: *Afflatus* has reportedly prompted poems, but it is *defenestration* that contributed to the starts of the Hussite Wars in the fifteenth century and the Thirty Years War in the seventeenth century in Prague. The Catholics thrown out the window in the second defenestration lived. Some say it was a miracle, and a message from God to the Protestants. Others say the Catholics survived because they landed in horse manure that softened their fall.

 # Math 101

The Bridges of Königsberg

The solution here is that there isn't a solution, and a mathematical proof can establish that. A Swiss mathematician, Leonhard Euler (1707–1783), proved that you could *not* cross all the bridges only once to complete the circuit of bridges and tour the city. His method of proof contributed greatly to graph theory and helped launch topology as an area of math. Euler was one of the eighteenth century's greatest mathematical minds, despite the fact that he was blind in one eye by his late twenties and completely blind for more than the last decade of his life.

{ fyi }

Since the bombings of WWII and subsequent modernization, only one of the seven Königsberg bridges from Euler's time is said to still exist.

The Four-Color Map Theorem

In the nineteenth century, someone proved that any map with countries of multiple adjacent borders could be colored with as few as five colors, but several efforts to prove it could be done with as few as *four* colors came up short. Finally, in 1976, using a computer to analyze almost two thousand maps, some mathematicians created a proof. This was the first theorem to be solved with computer assistance, which made the finding controversial, because it couldn't be validated by human calculations alone. Simpler proofs have since been presented.

 **Arts 101**

Screen Talk

1) *On the Waterfront*
2) *The Adventures of Sherlock Holmes*
3) *The Wizard of Oz*
4) *Sudden Impact*
5) *All the President's Men*
6) *Jerry Maguire*
7) *The Terminator*
8) *Field of Dreams*
9) *Star Wars*
10) *Casablanca*
11) *All That Jazz*
12) *The Godfather*
13) *Gone with the Wind*
14) *Poltergeist*
15) *Titanic*
16) *Taxi Driver*
17) *Lord of the Rings*
18) *Auntie Mame*
19) *Network*
20) *Dead Poet's Society*

Sculptural Stumper

1) Auguste Rodin
2) Franz Xaver Messerschmidt
3) Michelangelo Buonarroti
4) John Henry Foley
5) Frédéric-Auguste Bartholdi
6) Emmanuel Frémiet
7) Praxiteles

 # Social Studies 101

Big and Small

Throughout history, humans have carved up the earth's land, created boundaries on maps, and given names to defined areas. Here's the most recent "big and small" of it:

1) Five Largest Nations (measured by area in square miles)
   Russia: 6,592,849 square miles
   Canada: 3,851,809 square miles
   United States: 3,717,813 square miles
   China: 3,705,407 square miles
   Brazil: 3,286,488 square miles

2) Five Smallest Nations (measured by area in square miles)
   Vatican City: 0.17 square miles
   Monaco: 0.8 square miles
   Nauru: 8 square miles
   Tuvalu: 9 square miles
   San Marino: 24 square miles

3) The Size of the Natural World
   Total: approximately 316,944,046 square miles

4) Surface Area
   Land: 148.94 million square kilometers (29.2 percent of the earth's surface)
   Water: 361.132 million square kilometers (70.8 percent of the earth's surface)
   Coastline: 356,000 kilometers

 # Science 101

Who Are You?

If you have a backbone, you are a Chordate, along with fish, reptiles, birds, and mammals.

Index